MW01030220

Don't
T.E.L.L.
Me What To Do!

A Roadmap To Meaningful Client Conversations

Mike Milan

Cash Flow Mike

Copyright © 2024

All Rights Reserved

ISBN: 979-8-335327-57-2

Disclaimer

This book, including all content, insights, and advice, is provided for general informational purposes only and does not constitute financial, legal, or professional advice. While the author, Mike Milan, and all contributing parties have made every effort to ensure the accuracy and reliability of the information presented herein, the rapidly changing nature of financial laws, regulations, and market conditions means that the content may not reflect the most current developments.

The author and publisher expressly disclaim any and all liability concerning any action or inaction based on the contents of this book. Readers are encouraged to consult with professional advisors for advice concerning specific matters before making any decision, and the author and publisher cannot be held responsible for any loss, damage, or other issues that may arise from the use of the information contained in this book.

The anecdotes, case studies, and examples contained within are provided for illustrative purposes only and do not guarantee or predict any specific outcome for individual businesses or financial situations. Any trademarks, service marks, registered trademarks, or registered service marks mentioned in this book are the property of their respective owners and are mentioned for identification purposes only.

Implementing the strategies outlined in this book should be done with consideration of your personal or business financial situation, and with the understanding that the author and publisher are not providing tailored financial advice.

03

Acknowledgements

Well, folks, they say it takes a village, and they're not kidding. This book is standing tall today because of a bunch of people who've poured their wisdom, time, and faith into me and my wild ideas. First up, Larry Weinstein, CPA, CPCP – Larry, you're the real MVP for always nudging me to level up The Clear Path To Cash program. Your relentless push for greatness turned good into great, and for that, I owe you a truckload of thanks.

Then there's Don O'Dell, CPA, CPCP. Don, you've been the voice in my corner, the one telling me to take the leap and spread the word on having killer conversations that really move the needle. Your encouragement's been like jet fuel for my confidence.

And can't forget David "Stosh" Stauffacher, CPCP. Stosh, you believed in the way I break things down – simple, no fluff, just straight talk that gets results. Your confidence in my message made it resonate in ways I never imagined.

To every single soul in the Cash Flow Mike Clear Path To Cash community – you are the heartbeat of this journey. Every success story, every breakthrough, it's all you. This community, this family we've built, it's made my mission a heck of a lot more than just a job. It's a calling, and I'm grateful for every one of you who's joined this ride.

So, hats off and a massive thank you to each and every one of you who's played a part in this. Without you, these pages would be just that – pages. With you, they're a movement. Let's keep this train rolling.

Cash Flow Mike

About The Author
Cash Flow Mike

Mike Milan, better known to many as Cash Flow Mike, is the entrepreneurial force of nature with a knack for spinning plates that most folks wouldn't dare to touch. His resume? It's a wild mosaic, a testament to a life lived with gusto—a bit like jazz, full of improvisation and bold moves.

From the disciplined ranks of the Army National Guard and the front lines as a Missouri State Trooper to steering the ship of a 500-employee hotel staffing firm, Mike's done it all. He's poured drinks and crunched numbers as the owner of three bar/restaurants, played landlord with numerous rental properties, and even dabbled in herbal supplements, securing a spot in 119 Walgreens stores before learning some tough business lessons.

Mike's hands have been dipped in the concrete of construction for a major non-profit, and he's left his mark on the tech world with a financial software application designed for small businesses and accountants. When he's not leading coders or building things, he's sharing his art of financial management with thousands of bankers, accountants, and business owners, helping them find their own Clear Path To Cash.

An author of not one, but two books, "Don't Be D.U.M.B. Business Owner" and "The 7 Minute Conversation," Mike wields the pen with the same passion he brings to business. With an MBA from Baylor University tucked under his belt, he's as comfortable in the boardroom as he is on the open road—motorcycle throttled up, wind in his face, or sinking a putt on a serene green.

Mike's the proud dad to three daughters, each as awesome and beautiful as a Texas sunrise. And if that's not enough, he's also parachuted from planes, crafted poetry, and fallen in love with life over and over again. To meet Mike is to meet a whirlwind of experiences, a man who embraces life's peaks and valleys with the throttle wide open.

Buckle up; Cash Flow Mike's at the wheel, and the journey's just getting started.

Preface

I never imagined I'd write three books, but here we are. "Don't Tell Me What To Do: The Roadmap For Meaningful Client Conversations" isn't a manifesto from an ivory tower; it's forged from the trenches of real, gritty financial work. It all started in the classroom. I was teaching advisors how to integrate financial concepts into their businesses, but something wasn't clicking. They had the knowledge, sure, but their clients weren't truly committing to the necessary actions—they were just nodding along.

That's when it hit me: nobody likes being told what to do, myself included. It's human nature. And the more I pressed, the more resistance I felt. It was a breakthrough moment, realizing that our most impactful work doesn't happen in the glow of the computer screen, poring over financial plans. It happens in the connection we forge, the words we exchange with our clients.

Combining my frontline experiences with clients, the verbal judo techniques I learned as a state trooper, and yes, even the approaches I observed psychologists use on the TV show "Hoarders," I crafted The Elevation Sequence. This is more than just a method—it's a movement. It's about using the power of conversation to steer, not to control; to guide, not to dictate.

In these pages, you'll find not just the theories but the practical, battle-tested strategies that will help you transform your client conversations from monologues into dialogues, from transactions into partnerships. We're in this together—advisors, clients,

07

humans. And it's time we talk to each other in a way that gets things done.

In "Don't Tell Me What To Do", I delve into the art of getting clients to talk more by using effective conversation techniques, represented by the acronym T.E.L.L., which stands for Terminate Every Long Lecture. This strategy ensures that clients talk about 70% of the time, which is crucial for uncovering their real needs and concerns. This approach also ties seamlessly with the strategies I laid out in "Don't Be a D.U.M.B. Business Owner, (Don't Understand My Business)" where T.E.L.L. helps identify the issues, and D.U.M.B. provides the solutions. Together, these books equip advisors with the necessary tools to enhance client interactions, leading to more insightful discoveries and impactful solutions.

So, let's embark on this journey—not just to change how we talk, but to change how we think about talking. Let's create those meaningful conversations that inspire action and foster a deeper understanding. After all, the true measure of our success lies not just in the transferable value we create, but in the trust we build and the dreams we help realize.

Cash Flow Mike

TABLE OF CONTENTS

Introduction

Welcome to the crossroads of finance and conversation, where the spreadsheet meets the heart. In "Don't Tell Me What To Do! The Roadmap For Meaningful Client Conversations," we're flipping the script on traditional financial advising. Here, it's not just about the numbers—it's about the narratives behind them. The Elevation Sequence isn't your standard financial playbook; it's a journey into the art of conversation, a path I discovered while teaching advisors how to navigate the complexities of client relationships.

Recognizing that our industry needed more than just technical acumen, I saw the vital need for a framework that emphasized the person behind the portfolio. Just as physicians delve deeper than the symptoms to treat their patients, financial advisors must look beyond the balance sheet to understand their clients' stories, fears, and dreams.

We start with Harmony, where we establish a bond of trust, similar to a musical harmony that sets the tone for a great symphony. Using techniques like The Compass, we create dialogues that resonate with empathy and understanding, all with the end in mind. The Nudge Pact and Clear The Noise help us align our intentions with our clients', clearing the path for genuine discovery and collaboration.

As we delve into the Depth phase, we navigate the deeper currents of our clients' aspirations and barriers. The Explorer, The Crowbar, and The Mirror Moment are not just tools but bridges to a greater understanding, guiding our clients to insights that align with their true financial objectives. This is where a sensitive touch and strategic insight blend to lead our clients on a voyage of self-discovery and realization.

Then comes Elevate, the phase where we use the trust and insights we've built to chart a course toward action. Techniques like The Economic Echo and Accolade Anchor take center stage, transforming insights into strategies and past successes into motivation for future endeavors. This phase is where conversations evolve into concrete outcomes and life-changing results.

This book is more than a collection of strategies; it's an ethos that acknowledges the intertwined journey of financial and personal evolution. It challenges advisors to step up as not just wealth managers but as architects of their clients' broader ambitions. It's an invitation to elevate the advisor-client dialogue into an impactful exchange of ideas and aspirations. So, let's rewrite the narrative of financial advising together, one meaningful conversation at a time. Let's not just do business; let's inspire change and build legacies that last.

Welcome to the revolution. Welcome to "Don't Tell Me What To Do! The Roadmap For Meaningful Client Conversations." T.E.L.L being the key word in this concept. In my world, I think the client should be talking 70% of the time and the advisor talks for the remaining 30%. The acronym T.E.L.L. should be a reminder for you to:

TERMINATE EVERY LONG LECTURE

Let your client talk and work side by side with you. Here is how.

Cash Flow Mike

Cash FlowMike

Part-1
Harmony:
Cultivating
Connection

Let's take a moment to envision a scene that perfectly captures the essence of Harmony - Cultivating Connection, weaving together The Compass, The Nudge Pact, and Clear The Noise into a narrative that sets the stage for deep, impactful client conversations. The entire premise of this book is to help your clients commit to change, not just be compliant with your advice.

I had a session with Chris, a visionary with the spark of potential in his eyes but carrying the weight of past financial advisors that missed the mark. They always seemed to be more focused on sales pitches than on fueling his vision. He meets me on Zoom with a mix of hope and skepticism. He's ready for a new chapter yet bracing for the old song and dance.

This is where we flip the script.

I start with a question that sidesteps the usual preliminaries:

"Chris, let's paint the big picture. After you've closed this chapter of the business, what's the dream you're chasing next?"

This isn't just small talk. It's The Compass in action—aiming to understand Chris's true north, beyond the numbers. If you've studied The Clear Path To Cash, then you know, this is the first lesson – we are Starting With The End In Mind.

You can learn more about The Clear Path To Cash at my website: www.cashflowmike.com.

"Chris, you know, most folks I work with, we end up sticking together for the long haul. It's important I get the full picture, I need to know where we are going. What's the dream, Chris? Lay it on me. Because once I've got that, I can gear everything we do towards that North Star of yours."

And as Chris, momentarily caught off-guard, quickly warmed up to the conversation's turn, he began to outline his post-exit dream.

This is where we learn about the reason, he puts everything into his business - the aspirations that fuel his drive beyond the balance sheet. This is where I tune in with full attention. Because this, right here, is where we start laying down the bricks of trust, setting up for the long game, and turning those dreams into plans. More importantly, I now have the first piece in being able to motivate him when the work of transforming his company gets hard.

As our dialogue progresses, I introduce The Nudge Pact.

"Chris, as we chart this path together, there will be moments of challenge and hesitation. Times when you won't want to do the things we need to do next. Let me know what signs to look for that scream you need that extra nudge, that gentle push to leap into what's tough but necessary for your success."

This question is all about establishing a partnership where encouragement is tailored and timely, fostering a space where Chris feels empowered to move beyond his comfort zone. This is the time when you have to move from advisor to coach. Your client needs your help, that gentle nudge to be better.

But the journey of transformation isn't without its distractions and detours. This is where Clear The Noise comes into play.

"Chis, start us off – what's been going on in your world that we should talk about first?" I ask.

It's an invitation for Chris to voice the here-and-now worries that might derail his larger goals. This part of our conversation is crucial; it's about identifying and prioritizing the present issues that need our attention. It wouldn't do us any good to talk about anything on our agenda when they have something so heavy they are worried about.

Chris walked in with a wall up, your typical entrepreneur guarding his life's work like a dragon with its gold. But here's the thing – walls come down when trust builds up. Now, he's all in, sleeves rolled up, ready to craft the big dreams into bigger realities. And me? I'm not just some suit doling out advice; I'm the guy in the trenches with him, side by side, mapping out the moves that'll make his dreams click into place.

That's what we're doing here, laying down the tracks for the future. It's all about connection – real, solid, 'I've got your back' kind of stuff. With The Compass in hand, we're lining up our shots with the precision of a master archer, making sure we hit the bullseye of Chris's ambitions. Throw in The Nudge Pact for that kick of courage when the hill looks too steep and Clear The Noise to mute the static that life loves to crank up. That's the Harmony phase of our conversation in action, folks.

HARMONY

The Compass

Issue?

NO   YES

Clear The Noise   Clear Path To Cash

So, as you turn these pages, think about that initial impression that Chris had about me – another advisor. It's a reminder of what these conversations can do – they're not just talk, they're the very blueprint of success. From this

Issue?   YES

NO

DEPTH

initial meeting, the dynamic between Chris and I shifts profoundly.

15

Chapter One

BUILDING TRUST WITH
The Compass

Best used when: starting a financial discussion with a client, it's crucial to align their current concerns and long-term goals.

Alright, let's crack open the compass case and get down to brass tacks. This is where the rubber meets the road, the starting block of our marathon. Picture The Compass not just as a tool but as your secret weapon in the financial advisory game. It's about laying down the first cards, getting a good read on the lay of the land, and understanding the heartbeats behind those bank statements.

Think of yourself not just as a guide but as the lighthouse for your clients, shining a light on the path through the financial fog. The Compass is your first move, your opening gambit in the chess game of finance. It's where we get real, asking the kind of questions that peel back the layers to reveal what's ticking underneath. Where are your clients coming from, and where are they itching to go? This is where we tune in, setting up for a journey that's as unique as their financial DNA.

The real trick of The Compass isn't just its knack for breaking the ice; it's also

Building Trust with The Compass

how it charts the course for where we're headed. Whether I'm in the advisory seat for a year or a couple of decades, the journey's the same: we've got to set the right direction from the get-go. Because in the end, understanding the destination is crucial in making the right calls along the way. I don't just toss questions for the sake of filling the air; I'm looking to unlock the map to their goals, aspirations, and yes, even their concerns.

With The Compass in hand, I'm a co-navigator in the long-haul voyage of my client's business adventure. After all, we need to know where the client wants to go in order to help them navigate. When clients sit down with me, they know it's not a drive-thru consultation we're plotting a cross-country trip. And with every question, we're not just making small talk; we're drawing the map, marking the milestones, and tuning the route to their dreams. That's the Compass— it's not about where you are; it's about where you want to end up, and making sure every step we take is a step in the right direction.

My favorite way to start the conversation is with this introduction.

"Part of working with you is helping you do whatever it is you want to do next. Meaning after you leave this company behind. With that in mind, where are we going? What do you want to do next?"

This approach works because it immediately taps into the personal aspirations of the client, showing that you care about their life beyond the balance sheet. It sets a tone of partnership and long-term planning, framing your relationship as a means to support their broader dreams, not just their current business needs.

Besides, it totally floors them. No one ever asks them this question. The mediocre advisor just starts in with their step-by-step program, giving every client the exact same experience and advice.

By the way, this first few minutes of working with your client are the most crucial. It's the time when your client can be the most defensive. They don't know you or what is about to happen, so they have their guard up.

Just like in that first scene of "Hoarders," where the psychologist stands at the threshold with the homeowner, we stand at the doorway to change. Beyond the client's shoulder, we both see the tangle of challenges their business practices have knotted up. They're glaring, they're messy, and they can't be ignored.

The beauty of the psychologist's approach? It's all about dialing down the tension, cracking open the door to dialogue. They let the homeowner take the lead, share their story, and make sense of the mess. That's the art of easing into the tough stuff, and it's not much different in our advisor-client relationship. We see the chaos, the missteps in their business. But before we can dive in and declutter, we've got to grasp the why and the how of their situation.

So, here's where The Compass points us to some critical questions. Questions we can ask to open the conversation.

"Looking at how things are, can you walk me through the decisions that led us here?"

18

Building Trust with The Compass

"What's the one thing in your business that you wish you could overhaul?"

"How does this situation align with where you are wanting to go?

It's their moment to talk, to reflect, and in a way, to rationalize what's been happening in their business before we roll up our sleeves. It's about identifying the problems; it's understanding their roots— because that's where the real solutions begin.

Here's are some other examples of how we get the ball rolling with The Compass:

"Tell me what I'm looking at."

A straightforward invite for clients to share their view, to let us into their financial world as they see it.

"What do you think happened to get to this point?"

This nudges them to look back, offering insights into their financial journey and the choices that shaped their path.

"What's something you wished others would understand about this situation?"

This question recognizes the complexity of their experience, acknowledging their feelings and challenges.

"How can we explore this together, so you feel comfortable?"

It's our pledge for teamwork and mutual respect, making sure we're moving forward together in sync and with ease.

The Compass is about striking a chord of harmony right from the start, making sure the foundation of our advisor-client relationship is solid as a rock. It's in these opening exchanges that trust starts to build, fed by the genuine engagement and empathy we bring to the table.

As we dive into this chapter, keep in mind: mastering The Compass is like learning a new language—the language of listening, understanding, and aligning with your clients' deepest aspirations and dreams.

Our goal? To navigate not just through the spreadsheets but through the personal stories and ambitions of our clients, crafting a journey that's in tune with their true north.

The Importance of First Impressions

Alright, let's zoom in on the game-changer, the deal-breaker, the make-or-break moment in any relationship: first impressions. They say you never get a second chance to make one, and nowhere is this truer than in the world of financial advising. Let's dive into why nailing that first impression isn't just important—it's everything.

Building Trust with The Compass

Take the story of Chris, for instance. Chris jumped on a Zoom call with a mix of hope and caution, his past experiences with financial advisors leaving him more guarded than Fort Knox. This was my shot, not just to dazzle him with financial wizardry but to show him I'm in his corner—for real.

From the get-go, I threw the standard playbook out the window. Remember, successful advisors have to be chameleons. Instead of bombarding him with jargon or diving straight into the numbers, I started with a simple,

"Chris, where's this journey taking you?"

This wasn't about catching him off guard; it was about catching his story, his why, and his trust. And just like that, we were no longer just advisors and clients but co-navigators on his financial journey.

Now, let's flip the script and imagine what would have happened if I missed the mark on that crucial first impression. Picture Chris joining in, already skeptical, and me launching into a monologue about industry performance benchmarks and operational cash flow tactics without so much as a "Tell me about your vision." In this version, Chris glazes over with boredom, and I'm left talking to the walls. Why? Because I failed to acknowledge the person behind the company, to show that I see him, hear him, and value him—not just his business.

These two scenarios underscore the power of first impressions. They're our opening notes in the symphony of client relations, setting the tone for everything that follows. Nail it, and you open the door to trust, respect, and genuine connection. Flub it, and you might as well be climbing Everest in flip-flops—possible, but why make it so hard?

The Compass technique is our guiding star in crafting these pivotal moments. It's about starting the conversation with empathy, curiosity, and the kind of questions that show you're not just another advisor— they're in the presence of someone who genuinely cares about their story and their success. It's also the perfect place to transition to talking about financials and our reason for working together.

If you practice the concepts in The Clear Path To Cash, you know I'm talking about Start With The End In Mind. This technique converts our clients dream into a financial reality. The first step in working towards building real transferrable value with your business is set up perfectly with The Compass. You are now setting the stage for providing your client one number to focus on, like the lighthouse we need you to become.

Techniques for Engaging Empathetically

Rollup your sleeves, because we're diving deep into the art and soul of engaging empathetically with our clients. If first impressions are the handshake, empathetic engagement is the conversation that turns a

handshake into a hug. It's what transforms a professional exchange into a personal connection. And trust me, in the world of financial advising, this is where the magic happens.

Building Trust with The Compass

Let's circle back to Chris. Here's a guy who's seen it all—the good, the bad, and the ugly side of financial advice. When he first joined my program, his skepticism was as thick as a bank vault door. The challenge? To not just chip away at that skepticism but to replace it with trust, respect, and, yes, even a bit of admiration.

How do we do it? Through empathetic engagement.

Empathetic engagement isn't just about nodding at the right moments or tossing out a sympathetic smile. It's about diving into the deep end of understanding, swimming in the waters of your client's world, and surfacing with the treasures of their trust and respect. It's about asking the right questions—and actually caring about the answers.

For Chris, the transformation began the moment I decided to ask, "Tell me what I'm looking at from your perspective." It wasn't just a question; it was an invitation—an invitation to open up about his journey, his struggles, and his vision for the future. This question was my way of saying, "I see you, Chris. Not just the entrepreneur in front of me, but the person behind the business."

When we talk about transforming the advisor-client relationship, engaging empathetically is not just a strategy—it's the heart of the matter. Drawing from our deep dive with Chris, here are the essential techniques, framed as actionable insights, to make every financial conversation count.

Open With Invitation

Invite Their Perspective: Start by asking, "Tell me what I'm looking at from your perspective." This approach signals that you're not just interested in numbers but in their story and experiences.

Foster Reflection

Encourage Self-Reflection: Use questions like, "What do you think happened to get to this point?" to prompt clients to build self-awareness. It also forces them talk about it out loud. Remember, if they say it, it must be true. If you say it, they can argue about it.

Validate Their Experience

Acknowledge Their Unique Challenges: By asking, "What's something you wished others would understand about this situation?" you validate their experiences and creates a space where they feel seen and heard.

 Collaborate on Comfort

Build a Partnership: Ending with, "How can we explorethis together, so you feel comfortable?" establishes the advisory relationship as a partnership, where decisionsare made together,with mutual respect and understanding.

Building Trust with The Compass

The Power of Active Listening

Listen to Understand, Not to Respond: Active listening goes beyond hearing their words; it's about engaging with the emotions and intentions behind them. Show you're absorbing every detail. If there is a perfect mix in conversation, it's 70/30. With your client doing most of the talking.

Embrace Their Vision

Align with Their Goals: Understanding your client's goals—both personal and financial—is key. Align your advice and strategies with their broader life aspirations, making it clear that their success is your success.

Provide Tailored Guidance

Offer Customized Advice: Every client is unique, and so should be your guidance. Tailor your advice to fit their specific situation, demonstrating that you've not only listened but have also crafted solutions with their best interests at heart.

Maintain a Judgement-Free Zone

Create a Safe Space for Sharing: Ensure your clients feel comfortable sharing their thoughts and feelings without fear of judgment. A safe space encourages openness, fostering a deeper connection and understanding.

By incorporating these techniques into your interactions, you not only elevate the quality of your client relationships but also set the stage for a more fulfilling advisory experience. Nobody likes to be told what to do, so this technique lets them feel like they are in control of the conversation.

Case Study: Establishing Trust with a Skeptical Client

Let's get back into the world of Chris, our skeptical entrepreneur, to see The Compass technique in action and see how our conversation rolled out.

A New Chapter with Chris

Chris jumps onto Zoom. He's hopeful but also wary from his past disappointments. His history with financial advisors reads like a series of missed connections, each one adding another layer of armor around him. Today, he's braced for the same old pitch, the familiar dance around dollars and cents. Chris knows he needs help but comes to the table thinking only about the cost of the advisor.

Building Trust with The Compass

The Compass Unfolds

As we sit down, the air is thick with anticipation. I break the ice not with forecasts or financial models but with a simple,

"Chris, let's cut to the chase. When you think about success, what does that picture look like to you?"

It's an unexpected detour from the beaten path, and it catches Chris off guard.

Chris' Response

He pauses, eyeing me with a mix of curiosity and caution. Then, slowly, the walls begin to crumble.

"I guess I've never been asked that by a financial advisor before," he admits. *"For me, success isn't just about the balance in my bank account. It's about building something that lasts, something I can be proud of."*

This moment, this admission, is our first glimpse into the real Chris—not just the entrepreneur, but the dreamer, the builder, the legacy maker.

Engaging Deeper

Ok. Now I'm encouraged. I dig a little deeper.

"What led you to this point, Chris? What's the story behind the dream?"

This question invites him to share his journey, not just the highs and lows of entrepreneurship but the passion and purpose that fuel his venture. In every story there is a hero, and every hero has a purpose. What Chris and I need to do is to define his purpose. Why does he give everything to this business?

Chris leans in, and he's kind of enthusiastic. "It's been a rollercoaster, to be honest. But every decision, every setback, has been a lesson. I started this because I believed in doing things differently, in making a dent in the industry. When I leave this business, I want to be remembered as successful"

Validating and Collaborating

Listening to Chris, I nod, acknowledging the weight of his words. "It sounds like you've faced your fair share of challenges. I also know that I need a couple of more things from Chris before we can start.

Although Chris gave me a goal, it's way to vague. After all, what does "I want to be remembered as successful "mean? We can't work towards a goal that has no definition. I want to see him win, not just feel a certain way. So, we have to probe a little more.

"Chris, what does that mean, you want to be remembered as successful."

Building Trust with The Compass

"When you see yourself feeling successful in the future, what are you doing?"

This is the perfect opportunity to introduce Start With The End In Mind. If we can get him to visualize the things that he wants to do after he leaves this business, we can calculate a transferrable value amount to become our beacon for the future.

Chris says: "I'm sitting on the deck of my beach home, listening to the waves crash below and watching the sun go down." I respond with:

"Yes and imagine you and I are drinking a glass of wine, toasting to your success, and patting each other on the back. What had to happen for us to get there?"

Now, Chris is fully engaged, his initial skepticism replaced by a cautious optimism. "That's exactly what I'm looking for—someone who gets it, who sees beyond the spreadsheets to what I'm trying to build."

Conclusions Drawn from Chris's Case Study

Chris's genuine responses to our Compass-guided questions peel away the layers of doubt and open up a dialogue grounded in trust and mutual understanding. His answers reveal that The Compass technique helps bend any false beliefs that Chris had about financial advisors, and gets him focused on what matters most – his why. Why does he put everything into this business?

The Compass when coupled with Start With The End In Mind sets your advisory relationship off on the right foot. It also helps you

Building Trust with The Compass

focus your efforts on aligning your advice with the client's motivations.

- Personal Goals Over Pure Profit:

Chris's story reaffirms that success for clients often transcends financial gain. After all, who doesn't want to feel successful?

- The Power of the Journey:

Acknowledging the client's journey and envisioning what they're doing when they see themselves successful validates their experiences and builds a foundation of empathy and trust.

- Collaboration Is Key:

Engaging clients in a partnership, rather than a one-sided advisory relationship, empowers them to take active roles in their financial journey. Getting their buy-in is equivalent to getting results faster.

Chris's story show us that people need our help. In fact, they may have been looking for help for a long time. You have the perfect opportunity to show them that not all advisors are built the same. You are different. You help them see the future and walk the path beside them. Most importantly, they know you aren't there just to tell them what to do.

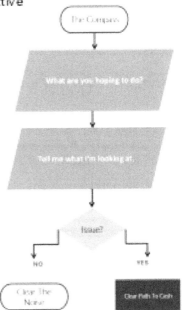

30

Chapter Two

MOTIVATING CLIENTS WITH
The Nudge Pact

Best used when: starting a financial discussion with a client, and to get them to act when they feel stuck. It's crucial to align their current concerns and long-term goals.

Step into the ring for the second round of our bout, and let's talk about The Nudge Pact: that subtle art of lighting a fire under someone, not to singe, but to warm up those gears of action. This isn't about barking orders or setting unrealistic targets. No, The Nudge Pact is like a dance, a two-step of trust and motivation between you and your client. It's about striking that sweet spot where "Maybe I should" or "I don't want to", transforms into "Let's roll up our sleeves and get this done."

The Gentle Art of The Nudge

The Nudge Pact isn't about strong-arming clients into action; it's that gentle jab at just the right moment. Think of it as that low-key, timely nudge that gets the gears turning again when they grind to a halt. We're talking about setting up a rhythm that moves to the same beat as their own drum – their hopes, their worries, and their 'what ifs.'

31

This isn't about giving orders. It's about locking arms and marching forward together. It's that nod we share that says, 'Hey, when the path gets a bit rocky, count on me to be your compass and your cheerleader.' When your client's looking at the mountain ahead, The Nudge Pact is your promise to hike it with them, step by step, to the peak of their goals. Let's face it. This is when you become the coach.

Crafting the Pact with Chris

Let's paint a picture with Chris as our muse. He's been down this road before, where promises were plenty but the follow-through? Not so much. Now, here he stands in our story, a little wary but open to a new chapter. We lay the groundwork for The Nudge Pact with some straight-shooting questions:

It starts out with an acknowledgment that even though finding issues and developing a plan might seem easy, the work isn't. Taking the right action to improve your company is uncomfortable. It's about breaking old habits and creating new ones. Bottom line is its work and at times you aren't going to want to do it. This is where an upfront agreement about how we act together is so critical.

"How will I know when you feel stuck?" I ask, looking him straight in the eye.

Motivating Clients with The Nudge Pact

"When I start to see that your stuck, think about getting a nudge from me, what do you think that looks like?"

This one's crucial. It's about personalizing your encouragement, tailoring it to suit their style, so it lands just right.

"What's worked best for you in the past for motivation?"

Here we're mining his history for nuggets of wisdom, past victories we can use as fuel for future triumphs.

"How do you see us tackling tough issues together?"

I'm not just offering a lifeline; I'm asking him to join me in tying the knots.

The Results Speak Volumes

The outcome? Chris, who once would balk at change, starts leaning into it. He's not just responding to the nudges; he's anticipating them, embracing them. Because now, he's not alone in this. He's got a co-conspirator in his corner, someone who's got his back, come hell or high water. He knows I'm not going to let him do nothing, hurting our chances to "feel successful" on the deck of his beach house in the future.

The Takeaway

The Nudge Pact isn't just about getting clients to act; it's about understanding the when, the how, and the why of their motivation. It's about turning the "I can't" into "We can," and transforming the solitary struggle into a shared adventure. The goal is to get their commitment to act, not just be compliant.

In the world of advising, it's easy to become the voice that's heard but not felt. The Nudge Pact changes the game. It turns us into the voice that whispers not just in their ears but in their hearts, saying, "I believe in you. Let's make this happen." There is a reason why we feel motivated to act. It's because the action directly connects to the reason you are doing it. Every time you have a task, it should be attached to a purpose.

In this chapter, we'll dissect every angle, pull at every thread, and show you how to weave The Nudge Pact into a safety net of trust and motivation. Get ready to turn those sparks of potential into a roaring blaze of action. This is where we make things happen, where we turn the "someday" into "starting now."

The recipe for success includes the coupling of the task and a purpose. In the Army, how do they get an 18 year old soldier to stand at a road intersection in a foreign country and stop traffic? They don't just give them an order. They explain "why" that action is important to the entire mission. They give the road intersection a purpose in the mind of the soldier.

If you want people to connect with you, to vote for you, buy from you, etc. Then they have to understand why it's important and beneficial. The Nudge Pact is your agreement with your client that the things you have asked them to do are both important and beneficial to creating transferrable value and their vision of the future.

Understanding Client Stagnation

Let's lay it out on the table: stagnation is like quicksand for the entrepreneurial spirit—it can suck you down and hold you fast, and the more you struggle on your own, the deeper you sink. The Nudge Pact is our strategic playbook for pulling clients out of the mire. This isn't about giving a pep talk; it's a tactical nudge that transforms "I'm stuck" into "I'm back on track."

Stagnation is a sly beast. It doesn't barge in; it creeps up, silent and unnoticed. One day you're moving full steam ahead, the next you're wondering why you're not moving at all. This is where I step in, not with a lifebuoy but with a question that's a lifeline: "How will I know when you feel stuck?" It's proactive, it's direct, and it cuts right to the chase. I'm not  waiting for the SOS; I'm on the lookout, ready to act.

The Nudge Pact in Motion

Let's break down the Nudge Pact with the fine-tooth comb of Chris's scenario. There's Chris, brilliant mind teeming with ideas, but he's hit a wall. Our session is spinning its wheels, and it's time for that pact we made, the one that nudges him from paralysis to progress.

Spotting the Signs: I ask Chris point-blank, "How will I know when you feel stuck?" It's a clear-cut pact—no fluff, just an honest commitment to signal when the going gets tough.Sometimes it won't be announced by Chris. He may shows signs like: not returning emails or calls, rescheduling meetings, or reluctance to take action by making excuses. When these things happen, we both know what is going on.

Tailoring the Push: "When you think about a nudge from me, how do you picture it?" I say. This is about Chris, his comfort zone, and how he wants that nudge to be delivered. It's personalized, respectful, and it shows I'm here to play by his rules. Plus, it helps you avoid the things he hates from someone trying to hold him accountable. He might not like feeling embarrassed, pressured, or small. It's about finding his motivation to act.

Learning from the Past: "What's worked best for you in the past?" I inquire. We're digging into his playbook of past victories, finding what strategy scored the winning touchdown so we can call that play again.

Approaching the Tough Stuff: "So, how do we face this giant challenge together?" I ask. It's about teaming up to build solutions, creating conversations that are about working side by side, not going head-to-head. It's more construction than confrontation.

Drawing Out the Stuck

These are the nuts and bolts of the Nudge Pact, the gears that turn stagnation into action. With Chris, each question is a step forward.

Motivating Clients with The Nudge Pact

They're not just questions they're keys that unlock the shackles of stagnation. They give Chris the freedom to maneuver.

Although we are talking about entering into The Nudge Pact up front in our relationship, it's important to know that this technique generally gets used anytime your client gets stuck. It's a framework for jumpstarting a stagnant client and re-energizing their enthusiasm to get things done. To do this effectively, consider a few guiding principles.

- **Proactivity Over Passivity:** By staying on the lookout for signs of Chris's stagnation, we're proactive, not reactive. It's the difference between catching a stumble and breaking a fall.

- **Personalization Over Generalization:** Understanding how Chris wants to be nudged means the push is always right—not too soft, not too hard. It's the Goldilocks zone of motivation.

- **History as the Blueprint for the Future:** Chris's past successes are the blueprint for his future breakthroughs. By revisiting what worked before, we're not reinventing the wheel; we're giving it a new spin.

- **Collaboration as the Foundation:** Tackling challenges isn't a solo mission; it's a joint venture. We're in the trenches together, mapping out the battle plan, side by side.

The Art of the Nudge

The Nudge Pact is like that gentle kick in the pants your clients need when they're knee-deep in the 'what-ifs' and 'but maybes'. It's setting up this unspoken agreement that says, "Hey, when you're stuck in the mud, I'm here to help pull you out."

Chris's leap from 'maybe later' to 'let's roll' isn't just some success story I like to brag about. It's proof that with the right approach—knowing just what makes your client tick, respecting how they tick, and coming at them as a partner, not a pusher—we can light a fire under the most frozen of feet. The Nudge Pact's our secret handshake that transforms a shrug into a nod, a hesitation into a heck-yeah. It's not about prodding; it's about powering up their drive so "maybe" turns into "absolutely, let's do this."

Strategies for Encouragement and Progress

When the going gets tough, the tough get a gentle nudge—not over the cliff, but back onto the path of progress. Here we're not just doling out high-fives and motivational posters. We're deploying strategies that transform the lead weights into helium balloons of encouragement. Let's dive into the nitty-gritty of how we do just that, drawing on everything we've got in our arsenal, including the insights gleaned from our buddy, Chris.

Custom Nudges

Every client's got their rhythm, and the nudge they need ain't one-size-fits-all. So I ask 'em straight up, "Chris, when it comes time for that gentle elbow from me, what are some things you would be doing that would be my

Motivating Clients with The Nudge Pact

signal?" It's about crafting that personal fit, like a tailor with his measuring tape, making sure the nudges its just right.

For a guy like Chris, it was all about reading the signs — maybe he starts missing our coffee chats, or his emails get short, a little on the snippy side. Those are my cues. It's not about waiting for the wheels to wobble; it's catching the wobble before it starts. That way, when I give Chris that nudge, it's not coming out of the blue—it's the very thing he's been missing - a hand on the back guiding him to the next milestone.

In the end, Chris told me he responded best to someone just being direct. Call him out on his B.S. As a former State Trooper, you know I don't have a problem with that!

Here were three tactics that you could use if you encountered a client like Chris. Every nudge begins the same way:

"Remember when you said that when I saw the signs it was ok to give you a nudge?"

Then follow it up with the tactic you both agreed on. Like this.

- *"Chris, I noticed we've missed our last two strategy sessions. Let's book a time now to regroup and refocus on your priorities. How does your schedule look?"*

- *"Been catching the edge in your emails, Chris. It tells me you're up against it and might need a sounding board. What's one thing on your plate right now that you wish you could hand off?"*

- *"I'm sensing some resistance, Chris, and it's not like you to hold*

back. Let's walk through what's on your mind and hash out the next steps. A fresh perspective might be just what we need to tackle this hurdle. When can we sit down and chat?"

Victory Recall

We all have our greatest hits—the moments when we knocked it out of the park. "What's worked best for you in the past for encouragement?" That's me, getting Chris to harness the power of his past to fuel future progress.

Cooperative Confrontation

Nobody likes to wrestle with the tough stuff alone. So, when I say, "How do you think we should approach challenging topics?" I'm extending a hand for a tag-team match against the heavyweight problems. It's about ensuring Chris doesn't face the music alone; we choreograph our moves together.

Unpacking the Toolbox

Now, let's unpack these strategies and see how they align with the ethos of the Nudge Pact:

- Anticipation Over Reaction: Chris learned that when he's feeling the inertia creeping in, I've already got my hand extended, ready to pull him up.

Motivating Clients with The Nudge Pact

- **Customization Is Key:** No cookie-cutter nudges here. For Chris, a personalized nudge, calling him out directly, was the difference between moving with confidence and standing still.

- **Leverage the Past:** We build the future on the foundation of the past. By revisiting what's spurred Chris into action before, we can recreate and amplify those conditions to propel him forward again.

- **Tandem Strategies:** Facing challenges is a duo, not a solo act. Chris and I plot our course through the trickiest terrains together, ensuring that every step taken is one we're both prepared for.

Chris's story isn't just a narrative; it's proof. Proof that with the right strategies, progress is inevitable. And the Nudge Pact? It's our commitment, our bond that says to every Chris out there: "You're not pushing that boulder up the hill alone. We're right here with you, giving it a nudge whenever you need it."

Case Study: Overcoming Client Inertia

Alright, picture this: Emma, a design agency owner, was at a crossroad, things weren't working, and she had to revamp her entire process. This included restructuring the staff and eliminating a job. This isn't just a tale of motivation; it's a masterclass in The Nudge Pact at work, and how you can of overcome inertia by leaning into fear and transforming it into momentum.

The Paralysis of Change

Emma's staring down the barrel of change, knowing full well her business needs a shake-up. Nobody ever looks forward to layoffs, but it was the one thing that meant her business lived or died. But here's the kicker—the thought of stirring the pot had her feet glued to the floor. She's frozen, not because she doubts the need for change, but because the thought of rattling her team's workflow has her breaking out in cold sweats.

The Nudge Pact Takes Center Stage

When you are working with a client, the telltale signs of a leader in limbo are hard to miss. It's time to wheel out The Nudge Pact.

Motivating Clients with The Nudge Pact

"Remember when you said if I saw you struggling, I could step in? What's got you worried about making these shifts?"

That question—it's a lance to the bubble of inertia. Emma opened up about her fears. She was worried about the ripples of change, and how it might throw her team's rhythm out of sync.

My next play was to join the team.

"What can I do to help make this change easier on your crew?"

Bam! That's not just a question; it's an alliance being formed, a promise that I'm in this trench with her.

The Strategy Unfolds

As Emma talked, I was listening—but I was also plotting, strategizing. I was looking at every hesitation, every flicker of doubt, and crafting it into a blueprint for action. This is The Nudge Pact dancing to life.

- **Understanding the Hesitation:** Keep your ear to the ground, listening to your client's concerns. It's empathy in action, the foundation stone of The Nudge Pact.

- **Personalizing the Support:** Emma's didn't get a one-size-fits-all solution. It's about making that nudge feel like it's got Emma's name on it.

- Drawing on the Past for Future Triumphs: We dove into what's worked before, using history as a guide for the moves they'll make. It's about repeating the wins, not the woes.

- Cooperative Approach to Challenge: This is the two of us, side by side, plotting a course through the minefield of change.

Breaking the Inertia

One of the things to remember about change is that people do not fear change, they fear loss.

With each exchange, each question, each collaborative plan, Emma's inertia started to crumble. She understood that we had to find a way to make the loss of a co-worker an opportunity to bond as a team. We devised a plan to include the remaining workforce in the redistribution of work, had regular check-ins planned, and made sure to celebrate every little success.

Feeling supported, she began to move. It's like the sun breaking through the clouds—suddenly, the path forward was clear, and she's ready to march down it. The most impactful thing we did was drawing out the process from beginning to end, before we set the plan in motion.

The Triumph of The Nudge Pact

Getting people to move is the raw power of The Nudge Pact kicking into high gear. It's about cracking the code of what makes a client stall, personalizing the pep talks, and getting down in the trenches together to map out a battle plan. This is where we transform a 'maybe tomorrow' into a 'heck yes, let's roll.'

Motivating Clients with The Nudge Pact

Call it The Nudge Pact, call it a secret weapon – whatever it is, it's practical magic for shaking off those doubts and getting down to business. Emma didn't just sidestep her fears; she blasted through them. It's all about hitting the gas when everything else says 'stop.' That's what happens when you pair up the right words with the right action.

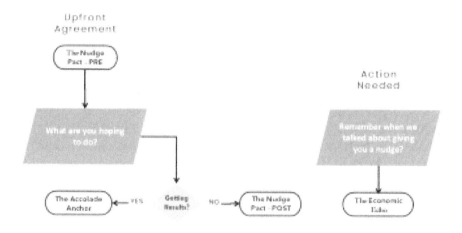

Chapter Three

IMMEDIATE CONCERNS FIRST
Clear The Noise

Best used when: starting a conversation and you want to take a moment to clear away irrelevant information and focus on essential points.

I magine you're in the eye of the storm, papers flying, phones ringing, and that little red dot blinking with a hundred urgent emails. That's where a lot of our clients are when they step into our world—swamped with the annoying noise of worries and what-ifs. That's where our strategy, Clear The Noise, comes in, wielding the volume knob of priorities like a maestro. It's about tuning into the right frequencies— the ones that matter right here, right now.

Dialing Down the Distractions

You will learn quickly that this will be your "go-to" question. I use it with every conversation, every engagement, and every group meeting. It cuts through the static the people have in their head. A simple question that frees your client's mind to really focus on the moment. It puts them in the place you need them to be to make real progress.

Immediate Concerns First Clear The Noise

When I ask clients like Sofia, "What's been going on in your world?" I'm not being nosy. I'm giving her permission to unload the baggage right at the onset so she can travel lighter through our meeting. It's about acknowledging that your client has a competing set of thoughts, things that keep them from fully committing to the conversation.

Setting the Stage for Success

"Is there anything you want to air out before we dive in?"

You just never know what battle your client is fighting the moment they step into a meeting with you. I know you as the advisor have an agenda, a purpose for the meeting. But this is where the saying: "Planning is everything, but the plan is nothing," comes into play.

You should have a plan, but the client might have a "burning issue". A problem that they think is on fire and needs immediate attention. A burning issue is one that is always the priority. It consumes their thoughts, time, and attention. If you ignore it, you have just wasted everyone's time. It's time to drop your plan and work on the thing that has

them worried first. This is me, helping the client to put up those blinders, so all they see is the finish line, not the hurdles, not the distractions.

47

The Outcome

By the time Sofia answers these types of questions, she's not just unburdened; she's laser focused. We've muted the background noise, and the only sound left is the clear voice of her goals calling.

Clearing The Path to Focus

You know, every client walks into a meeting lugging a suitcase full of 'what's on my mind today.' It's our job as advisors to unpack that suitcase first, no matter the game plan we've got scribbled down. Because whatever's eating up their brain space, that's the real priority. It's about tossing out the agenda when you need to because their immediate concerns — those are the real elephants in the room that need addressing.

Clear The Noise: The Present Meets the Future

Clear The Noise — it's not just about what's right in front of us; it's about scouting out the road ahead. We peel away all the layers of 'should-do's' and 'could-do's' until we're staring at the straight-up 'must-do's.' It's not about just quieting the racket for today; it's about laying down the tracks for tomorrow's train. We give room to air out today's hassles, and that's how we cut through the fog to the heart of what's next.

What is interesting is that if you make it a part of every occasion, your client grows to expect it. They might even initiate the meeting with statements like: "Can I clear some noise?" That is when you know you are providing real value. They feel heard. More importantly, they feel like you can help. You are an important part of their team.

Immediate Concerns First Clear The Noise

The Real Deal with Clear The Noise

So, here's the thing: amid the daily grind, with all its noise and bluster, our real gig is to zero in – laser-like – on the stuff that counts. Clear The Noise is our way of turning a jumble into a strategy, a to-do list into a success story. From that laser focus, we step forward into the big plays, the moves that count. That's the secret sauce to setting priorities, making strides, and, you bet, launching our clients towards the success they've been hustling for.

Addressing Current Concerns

Let's turn the spotlight on the challenge that haunts every boardroom and corner office—the current concerns that can drown out the sound of progress. It's the mental static that keeps our clients up at night, the nagging doubts and the day-to-day drags that can yank the focus away from the big picture. This is where our 'Clear The Noise' technique steps up to the plate, ready to knock these distractions out of the park.

The Straight Talk on Cutting Through the Clutter

Sofia is knee-deep in the hustle, with every little part of her business shouting for the spotlight. It's like every problem's got a megaphone, and the real deal issues? They're getting

drowned out. That's where 'Clear The Noise' steps in – it's our way of turning down the volume on the small stuff, so the big stuff gets its due.

The Fine Art of Tuning In

Here's how we work the magic:

- Lending an Ear: "What's been going on in your world lately?" This isn't idle chit chat; it's strategic. By opening the floor for Sofia to spill the beans on what's pressing, we're tuning our ears to the her concerns, filtering out the buzz so we can hear the matters that need our attention.

- Peeling Back Layers: "What's been keeping you awake?" By asking this, we're not just scratching the surface; we're peeling back the layers to reveal the raw spots, the irritations that could fester if left unaddressed. It's a gentle probe that shows we're here to help with their biggest problems.

- Creating a Safe Space: "Anything you need to get off your chest before we dive in?" This is about creating a safe zone where Sofia can declutter her mind, offloading the baggage that could stop us from working on building transferrable value.

Cranking Up the Clarity

The 'Clear The Noise' technique isn't just about listening; it's about understanding and action. It's a multi-tool that does more than just address the concerns at hand:

- **Strategic Sifting:** We sift through the worries and wonders, prioritizing the problems that pack a punch while setting aside the trivialities that can be tackled later.

- **Pinpointing Priorities:** "What's the headline for you right now?" We home in on what matters most to Sofia, the priority that deserves the spotlight. We gotta clear the deck of whatever's buzzing around in the client's head, or we'll just be adding more noise. Until we do that, there's no point in diving into our agenda – they won't hear a word of it over their own racket.

Turning Distractions into Directions

By addressing each concern, we're not just clearing the noise; we are dialing the pure sound of focus—Sofia's focus. This is where her business needs to steer next. It is what the business demands from her leadership, and where our advisory can support.

Clearing Mental Clutter for Clarity

One of the most critical challenges we face in the advisory world is sifting through mental clutter.

Clear The Noise is a technique I live by, in every ring I step into. Whether I'm steering a group coaching session, firing up the crowd at a live seminar, or just kicking back with friends, it's my go-to move. I lay out the landscape right from the get-go, so, everyone knows what's coming.

like when the next break is. It sets the stage, clears the air of any 'whens' or 'whats', and gets everybody locked in. It's about giving folks the comfort of knowing the play before the ball's even snapped – because when people know the plan, they're free to focus on the here and now without the background hum of the unknown.

Sifting Through The Static

Think about that one drawer everyone has at home, the "junk drawer," overstuffed with old batteries, expired coupons, and keys to forgotten locks. The mind can become just like that drawer, crammed with so much stuff that finding what you need becomes an expedition. Here's how we declutter the junk drawer of the mind to find the gold.

The Strategy: Precision Questioning

- Direct Inquiry: "What's been crowding your headspace lately?" That's me, asking Sofia to lay it all out on the table. It's not prying; it's prompting—a nudge to get her to unpack the clutter right there and then.

- Emotional Unpacking: "What's been keeping you up at night?" This one cuts deeper. We're not talking business operations; we're talking fears, hopes, dreams—because that's where the real clutter lies. It's the stuff that clouds judgment and clogs up the works.

52

Immediate Concerns First Clear The Noise

- Priority Check: "If you had to pick one thing that's taking up too much room up there, what would it be?" This question is the scalpel that excises the unnecessary, leaving us with the priorities that deserve the limelight.

The Toolbox: Techniques for Clarity

Once we've identified the clutter, we've got to deal with it. Here's the toolkit we deploy:

- Mind Mapping: Picture this - we grab all those swirling thoughts out of the ether and slap 'em on the wall. We're drawing lines, making connections, seeing the big picture. It's like taking a snapshot of a hurricane – suddenly, you see the eye in the middle of the storm.

- The Distraction List: We jot down every little gremlin that's been gnawing at the client's focus – the small stuff that's been nipping at their heels. Scribble them down, and it's like hitting the refresh button. Now, there's room to think, room to move, room to breathe.

- The Focus Funnel: A Focus Funnel is a strategic tool designed to streamline your tasks and priorities, ensuring you concentrate only on what truly drives your business forward. Start by listing all your tasks, then categorize them based on urgency and importance. Filter out the distractions and non-essentials, delegating or discarding what doesn't contribute directly to your goals. Prioritize the remaining tasks based on their impact, creating a refined list of high-value actions. Focus your energy on these prioritized tasks, ensuring your efforts are aligned with achieving significant results.

53

Harnessing Focus

Now, with the clutter in the rear view, we give Sofia the tools to maintain that clarity:

Routine Resets: We establish routines that routinely clear the clutter —weekly check-ins where we dump the drawer and sort it anew.

"What's one small thing we can check in on each week to keep our goals clear and your headspace clean?"

Decision Filters: Every new task or worry is run through a filter: Does this align with our key objectives? If not, it's put aside for later review.

"Does this get us closer to where you want to be, or is it just noise we should mute for now?"

Mindfulness Moments: We encourage Sofia to take intentional breaks, mental timeouts, to step back from the canvas so she doesn't get lost in the paint splotches.

"When was the last time you stepped back to clear your mind and look at the bigger picture?"

There's something about stepping back from the grind, you know? When the day's a blur of calls, meetings, and the endless tap of the keyboard, the best ideas – the real gems – don't always get a chance to shine. That's why I swear by mental timeouts. When I hit pause, take a walk outside in the yard, or just lay down for some shut-eye, it's like my mind shifts gears. Away from the noise, it starts working on another level, sifting through the day's puzzles. And more often than not, I wake up or walk back in with that 'aha' moment in my pocket, the answer that was hiding in plain sight all along. It's about giving your brain the space to breathe– that's when it does its best work.

The Payoff: Clarity in Decision Making

With these strategies, we're not just talking about a clear head; we're enabling a clear path forward. Sofia can now navigate her business waters not by dodging icebergs of distraction but by sailing straight and true to her destination.

By wielding these tools, by regularly clearing the mental clutter, we ensure that the decisions made aren't knee-jerk reactions to the noise, but responses to the music of Sofia's business vision. And that, my friends, is the sweet sound of success.

Case Study: Prioritizing Client Issues

Sofia is at a cluttered crossroads, her desk a chaotic mosaic of business strategies, each one louder than the last. Enter the 'Clear The Noise' technique. Things are about to get real clear, real fast.

Clear The Noise Technique Makes Decisions Easy

I sat down with Sofia, strategies strewn everywhere, each vying for her attention. It's obvious she can't decide on the direction the company needs to go. Heck, I'm confused too looking at her options. I change the direction of the conversation with one question.

55

"Out of these moves, which one's singing or talking to you the loudest?"

It's not just a question; it's a filter, cutting through the clutter to find the signal.

Sofia's Shift

Sofia, initially overwhelmed, starts to sift through the strategies. "What's the main area you'd like to see growth in over the next quarter?" I asked. With each question, Sofia's vision sharpens, like a photo coming into focus. Her resources, once scattered, align with laser precision on the strategies that matter.

She identifies three competing strategies: expanding the product line, investing in a new marketing campaign, and improving customer service. As we delve deeper, it becomes clear that while expanding the product line and marketing campaign have potential, they require significant investment and carry higher risk. On the other hand, improving customer service not only aligns closely with her current resources but also promises to enhance customer loyalty and drive sales growth more reliably. This strategy stands out as the obvious choice, offering a balanced approach to achieving sustainable growth.

The Clarity Effect

- Focused Strategy: With a nudge, Sofia narrows down her focus to the strategies that truly align with her business goals, leading to a surge in efficiency and market presence.

56

Immediate Concerns First Clear The Noise

- **Resource Alignment:** Resources are finite. 'Clear The Noise' helps Sofia direct her time, talent, and treasure toward actions that fuel her business's growth engine.

- **Decision Confidence:** Now, decisions are made not out of confusion but out of clarity. Each choice is intentional, impactful, and, most importantly, in line with her objectives.

The Contrast: The Perils of Untamed Noise

Imagine a universe where the noise never clears. Sofia's decisions become shots in the dark, her resources spread too thin. The team's morale drops under the weight of ever-shifting strategies, and business growth stutters in the static.

- **Scattergun Approach:** Without 'Clear The Noise,' Sofia's approach to grow this scattershot, lacking precision and focus.

- **Diminished Morale:** Teams thrive on clear direction. A leader lost in the noise breeds a team adrift, leading to decreased productivity.

- **Stunted Growth:** A business pulled in multiple directions grows nowhere. Opportunities are missed, and potential remains just that—potential, unfulfilled.

The Silence That Speaks Volumes

This case study isn't just about the success of one client; it's a blueprint for business sanity. 'Clear The Noise' isn't just a technique; it's a lifeline. It pulls leaders out of indecision and plants them firmly on solid ground with focused action.

This isn't just a clear path for Sofia; it's a lesson in business hygiene. It's a routine clean-up of the mental workspace, turning chaos into clarity, and clarity into success.

And that, folks, is the power of 'Clear The Noise.' It's the difference between a strategy that sings and one that sinks, between a business leader who leads and one who merely lingers.

Man, I'm getting good at creating contrast in a sentence to paint a picture!

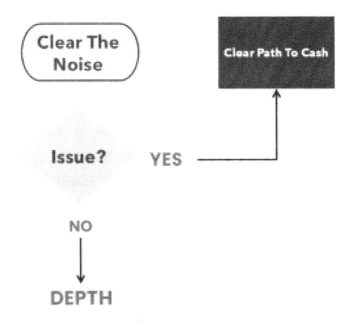

Cash Flow Mike

Part-2
Depth:

Discovering
The Undercurrents

59

In part-1, we were dealing with initial client interactions. Now, we go beyond the surface and into the essence of our clients' visions, their businesses, their very motivations. This is where the advisor makes their money. It's where what's unsaid often speaks louder than words, and where the core of future success lies hidden, waiting to be revealed.

Let's talk about Theo, a friend of mine who owned a restaurant. He was amazing at adding flavor in the kitchen, but his marketing strategy was super bland. He's the embodiment of The Explorer, a client who's current efforts are the tip of the iceberg, beneath which lies a wealth of unutilized potential and unrecognized obstacles.

Theo came to me frustrated. He just could not crack the code to creating a marketing message that delivered results. I let him vent and tell me about all of the money and time he wasted on experts and platforms. One thing is for sure, when your client starts to rant, let them go for a bit. Doesn't leap into solution mode. More often than not, they will talk around the problem and relive the emotion. So, after a few minutes of complaining about results, I ask a simple question.

"Tell me more about your current marketing."

It's the opening note of a deeper conversation, and as Theo unfolds his story, I gently probe beneath the layers, unveiling the disconnect between his vibrant culinary experiences and the bland messaging that fails to capture them.

Theo felt like the problem was within his marketing message. This narrows our focus quite a bit, but sometimes, the client just can't articulate where the problem might be. In this case, we need to use something a little stronger. I call it The Crowbar. It's purpose is to identify a theme in your client's answers. We'll see The Crowbar at work with Daniel, whose tech firm's innovation has flatlined. With my help, he learned that some questions act as a lever, prying open the sealed sections of his company's financial heart. The Crowbar exposes the root causes, the fuzzy areas that need sharpening, the gaps in their innovation pipeline that need filling and forces a clients to look at his business from several different angles at once.

The last technique in the Depth phase is The Mirror Moment. In some cases, like with Elena, whose boutique had a history of inconsistent sales. We learn that Elena couldn't see that she was part of the problem. It's one of those times when you have to take a delicate approach to showing the client what they look like In the mirror.

Sometimes you have to hold up the mirror with questions that encourage self-awareness and accountability. "What stands out to you about the feedback from your team?" As Elena contemplated the question, she was encouraged to look deeper, to truly see the reflection of her actions in the shop's performance, leading to a moment of clarity that changed everything.

In the Depth phase, we're doing way more than just nodding along – we're digging in, getting our hands dirty to uncover the gold. Think of us as the Indiana Jones of finance – we're on a quest through the thick jungle of numbers to unearth the hidden gems of our clients' deepest goals and gnarliest challenges. Tales like those of Theo, Daniel, and Elena? They're not just stories. They're the X marks the spot on the map of their business's wildest possibilities.

Each of the techniques in the Depth phase are all designed to do one thing. Find the issue that you can address using one of the techniques in The Clear Path To Cash. This is problem identification at it's finest, and one of your most powerful tools in attracting and retaining clients in your advisory services practice.

For more information about The Clear Path To Cash, check out my book titled: "Don't Be A D.U.M.B. (Don't Understand My Business) Business Owner". It can be found on Amazon or Barnes and Noble.

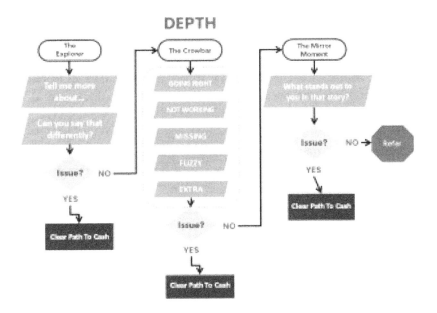

Chapter Four

UNVEILING
The Explorer

Best Used When: starting a conversation and you want to take a moment to clear away irrelevant information and focus on essential points.

R emember Theo, a maestro in the kitchen with a knack for creating flavors that could spin tales all by themselves. But, his marketing strategy was like an unseasoned bowl of cooked spaghetti– all the potential in the world, yet waiting for the right sauce to bring it to life.

Theo was so frustrated that it was blocking the path to his restaurant's success. It hovered over his every decision, a constant reminder that despite his efforts, the throngs of customers he envisioned remain just that—a vision.

"Tell me more about your current marketing efforts."

It's not just an opening question; it's the first step on a journey. As Theo speaks, his narrative meanders through tactics and attempts, each one revealing more about what isn't being said than what is.

"Why aren't folks flocking in?"

I'm not one to always buy the first excuse that comes up. Theo fumbles through an answer, tripping over reasons he hadn't even seen yet. Just like when I was a State Trooper, a person's real trouble is sometimes more clearly spelled out in every hesitation and deep sigh more than the words he's trying to string together.

As Theo struggled, I changed tactics and asked.

"Can you describe your strategy in a different way?"

It's a lifeline, pulling Theo from his own familiar thoughts into a new clarity of expression.

"What were you hoping would happen?"

This is where aspiration met reality. Theo's vision for his restaurant, for the ambience he wanted to create, the experience he wanted his customers to have came back to life.

With The Explorer technique, Theo started to see his marketing not just as a series of actions but as a narrative—a story he's telling the world about his restaurant. And somewhere between my questions and Theo's answers, a new strategy begins to take shape, one that's more in tune with the soul of his business.

This chapter kicks off Theo's big turnaround, the kind of comeback story we all root for. By asking the tough questions, Theo started sifting through the noise in his head to remember what made his restaurant special to begin with. This is where the magic happens: where what's left unsaid gets a voice, where the blurred vision sharpens into focus, and where a once-dusty marketing strategy rises up, ready to take on the world.

Probing Beneath The Surface

Theo's situation underscores a fundamental principle: understanding a client's situation requires digging deeper than the surface-level symptoms of a problem. It's about engaging in a conversation that moves beyond the obvious to uncover the underlying issues affecting a client's progress.

Although I focus on the financial performance of a company, I realize that the actions powered by either motivation or frustration fuel the engine of their dream. I didn't solve a marketing problem, I just asked the right questions to get Theo to adjust his approach.

Applying the Explorer Technique

- Open-Ended Inquiry: I began with, "Tell me more about your current marketing efforts." This invitation for Theo to elaborate and vent creates an opening for deeper exploration, setting the stage for discovery.

- Seeking Root Causes: By asking, "Why do you think these efforts aren't attracting customers?" Theo is encouraged to analyze and reflect on the underlying reasons behind his marketing strategy's lackluster performance. This isn't just about what's happening; it's about understanding why it's happening.

- Encouraging Different Perspectives: "Can you describe your strategy in a different way?" This question forces Theo to reframe his approach, offering new angles and insights into his methods and objectives. It's a technique that fosters creative thinking and problem-solving.

- Aligning Expectations with Reality: "What were you hoping would happen?" By aligning Theo's expectations with the outcomes of his efforts, I helped him identify discrepancies and misalignments in his strategy, providing a clear direction for adjustment.

The Impact of Probing

Digging through the details, Theo starts seeing things in a whole new light—like flipping on the high beams on a foggy night. It ain't about serving up all the answers on a silver platter; it's about lobbing the right questions so Theo can hit 'em out of the park. This deep dive does more than just straighten out a few crooked signs; it syncs up Theo's fire for his food joint with the kind of game plan that gets folks talking. It's not just a marketing fix—it's about cooking up a vibe that Theo's place serves up something special.

Most importantly, Theo came up with it! I may have guided him to a logical conclusion, but getting Theo to say the words is the key to problem solving as an advisory. If I say it, Theo can push back and argue. If he says it, well... It must be true. After all, nobody likes to be told what to do. Wink wink.

The Contrast: What Happens without The Explorer

Sticking to just the financial end of marketing might've given Theo's place a bit of a boost, sure. We can evaluate Cost of Acquiring Customers (CAC) or Return on Ad Spend (ROAS). But that's small potatoes. It wouldn't have gotten to the heart of the mismatch between what Theo's got cookin' in his head and what he's got written in his ads. We went deeper and gave his restaurant more meaning than a plate of food as a discounted price. We gave people a reason to want to spend time with Theo. We connected to a bigger problem than hunger. We connected with a dining experience to remember.

The Outcome of the Explorer

Using The Explorer technique isn't just about scratching the surface; it's about tunneling to the core. We're talking deep, meaningful conversation that sparks those 'aha' moments, leading to the kind of strategies that click perfectly with what the client's really shooting for. It's about more than just quickly solving a problem—it's about unlocking your client's knowledge of their business that pave the way for real change and the kind of success that sticks.

Techniques for Deeper Inquiry

Let's unfold the layers of The Explorer technique, a method that's about much more than just scratching the surface. It's the fine art of of asking the kind of questions that dig deeper, to reveal the core beneath the client's story.

The Art of Open-Ended Inquiry

The first tool in our excavation kit is the open-ended inquiry. "Tell me more about the situation," serves as more of an invitation than a question. It opens the door to the client's thoughts and feelings, allowing them to lead the way into their inner world. This isn't about leading the witness; it's about following them into the depths, letting them guide you to the heart of their concerns. It's useful because it places the client in the driver's seat, allowing them to steer the conversation towards what really matters to them.

Seeking Root Causes

"Why do you think that is happening?" This question is like the pickaxe that cracks open the rock to reveal the gems inside.

It moves beyond the what and the how, asking for the why. This is where we begin to see the outlines of the root causes that are driving the problem. It forces the client to find causes, more than  recite the effects of the problem. Saying the cause out loud has a weird way of also highlighting a solution.

Unveiling The Explorer

Encouraging Different Perspectives

"Can you say that differently?" might seem like a simple request for clarification, but its implications run deep. It's a subtle nudge for the client to reframe their narrative, to look at their situation from a new angle. This technique is invaluable because it disrupts the habit your client has created in talking about the problem. The small exercise of having to restate the problem with different words often reveals solutions that were hidden in plain sight.

Aligning Expectations with Reality

"What were you hoping would happen?" This question bridges the gap between "smoking hope-ium" and reality. It's not just about identifying what went wrong; it's about understanding what the client hoped would go right. The power of this question lies in its ability to show the differences between expectations and outcomes, providing a clear direction for problem solving. Sometimes we mis-align our dream with our reality. "We can't get there from here." We can't buy a bus ticket to Fiji, even though both things seem to exist.

The Impact of Deep Inquiry

Rolling out these tools, we're setting up a whole new playing field—it's like flipping on the floodlights in a stadium. It isn't just about Theo spilling the beans on his business woes. It's about kick-starting his own thoughts. Suddenly, he's seeing the big picture—spotting patterns in the wilderness. There is

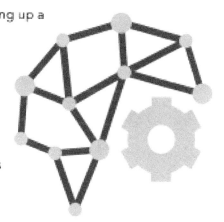

order in chaos if we are looking for it.

This deep dive is golden, not because it pops out quick fixes, but because it arms Theo with the kind of sharp insight that lets him chart his own course. We're creating a joint venture, where each of you are bringing your unique skills to the table. He knows restaurants, and you know how to find and solve business problems. You are an unbeatable team. A connection we can't live without.

The Outcome of Deep Inquiry

The Explorer method is a philosophy, a way of engaging with clients that respects their knowledge and autonomy while guiding them to deeper insights about their situation. It's about building a partnership based on mutual exploration and discovery, one where the answers come from within the client, illuminated by the careful, considered probing of the advisor. This is the essence of meaningful client conversations. Conversations that create a bond between you and your client that become non-negotiable. It a joint venture between their knowledge and yours. A partnership that breaks barriers.

70

Case Study: Revealing a Client's Unacknowledged Obstacles

Theo's restaurant is hidden in one of our larger cities. If you find it, you'll experience the aroma of exotic spices, warm lighting, soft ambient music and the clatter of a vibrant kitchen. Notice the word hidden and if you find it? Theo's marketing efforts are as effective as a blunt knife. His attempt to copy his competitor's ad copy and discounts just haven't worked.

The Story Unfolds

Theo met with me with a mix of hope and desperation. He was frustrated because his efforts to draw in crowds had fallen flat. His frustration only became worse as he thought about all the success everyone else was having. Why wasn't it happening for him?

The Explorer in Action

- Open-Ended Inquiry: After listening to his story, I asked, "Tell me more about your current marketing efforts." This question is crucial. It's an invitation for Theo to start telling me the story of what happened and why he feels the way that he does. Plus, he

- gets to vent a little. You want your client to have this space. Frustration needs an outlet, and you are in the best position in his life to provide it.

Theo went on to tell me about several promotions he had run, and about hiring "industry marketing experts" to turn his traffic count around. In reality, he ended up looking like every other restaurant in the area. He was a carbon copy of 4 other places in the same 2 block area. In fact, he was at an even bigger disadvantage. He was the farthest walk from the closest parking garage in the neighborhood. That was not what he needed at all. He needed to be himself and be different.

- **Seeking Root Causes:** "Why do you think these efforts aren't attracting customers?" I dig a little deeper, seeking the underbelly of Theo's strategy, nudging him to consider not just the what but the why of his failures.

This was a tough question for Theo. He blamed the marketing company, the photos, the price point. But he never thought about the idea that he was trying to blend in, believing that success was a formula that only others knew about.

- **Encouraging Different Perspectives:** "Can you describe your strategy in a different way?" Theo gets the chance to pivot, to view his strategy through a different lens. This question challenges him to distill his complex efforts into clearer, more concise terms. It is also designed to help you break free of any entrenched views he holds onto.

What ended up happening was that Theo instantly saw that he wasn't describing his restaurant at all. He was describing the

Unveiling The Explorer

marketing strategy that everyone else was using. When I asked, the next question it made a lot more sense to him.

- Aligning Expectations with Reality: "What were you hoping would happen?" This question bridges Theo's expectations with the stark reality of his outcomes, shedding light on the gap between his dreams and his reality.

Theo stated that he followed everyone else's lead and became just like everyone else. He wasn't unique, different, something to tell others about. He was the same – on paper. It was then, he realized that the cost of trying a restaurant that's the "same" as the one I currently frequent is too high. People will try new or different. They shy away from the same.

The Revelations

Theo's dive into the deep end shined a light on what real digging can do. It's solid proof that when you really can't get why things are falling flat, flip the script to see them differently. More times than not the big problem will become a lot clearer. And it's always easier to solve a problem when you can clearly define it.

This isn't just a tale of untangling knots; it's the master plan for spotting the hidden snags. Those questions, as simple as they look or sound, can unlock the obstacles that are keeping your client for taking the right action. It's a simple tool, that moves you from average advisor to can't live without confidant.

In Theo's case, it moved him from just like the others, to an experience you want to tell others about. He turned the disadvantage into a challenge. Even though he was the furthest from the parking garage, he included in all of his marketing: "It's worth the walk."

The Contrast: A Path Untaken

What if I skipped The Explorer, and like his marketing companies, I just tossed Theo cookie-cutter advice? Then I keep Theo stuck running circles in his own maze, firing off marketing duds one after the other—each miss eating away at his mojo and his budget.

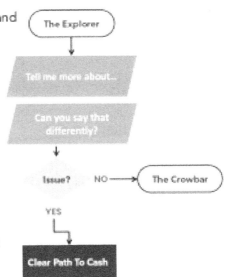

Instead, I helped Theo solve his own problem in a unique and effective way. Not only that, but we also got results. Now that's the best way to build a bond with your client!

Chapter Five

UNEARTH CORE ISSUES
The Crowbar

Best Used When: faced with persistent tough challenges or client resistance, it's time to dig deeper into the root causes behind the issues at hand.

In the nitty-gritty tango of business strategy and cash flow management, the biggest leaps often come from digging up the game-changing truths that are tucked away under daily grind and tough-to-crack habits. That's when I use The Crowbar– it's not just any old tool, but one for people set on busting through what's bogging them down and cutting straight to the core issue.

When I was in Seattle, I worked Daniel as they struggle with a tech company that was stuck in the mud. We weren't just looking to kickstart Daniel's business; we were on the hunt for the buried issues that got them stuck in the first place.

The Need for The Crowbar

Daniel's company, once known for breaking the mold, now finds itself lost in 'good enough' and mixed messages. Its once-clear path to market leadership got derailed by months of complacency and unclear directives. The biggest problem was Daniel. He couldn't

75

see or articulate any issues that were present in his company. He was vague and danced around from problem to problem. He never really could see the problem clear enough to build a strategy to correct it. It is cases like this where using The Crowbar in our conversation isn't merely a choice; it's a necessity. It's the tool I thought would help us pry open the sealed aspects of the company's strategy and culture that were hurting the mission.

The Process of Deep Excavation

The Crowbar isn't about just tossing out any tough questions; it's a precision tool, targeting the heart of a business's pain points. It's about lining up a very specific set of five key questions, each one forces your client to look at their business from all angles. These aren't random shots in the dark; they're calculated, aimed at drawing out patterns, and highlighting the themes that show where the biggest issues might be hiding.

So, this chapter, is not your average patch job. It's a deep dive that takes a little bit of time to dig into the foundation. With every question of The Crowbar, we are chipping away at the surface. They're mining for the kind of hard-hitting truths that shakeup the status quo and pave the way for solid, substantial rebuilds.

The Art of Challenging Questions

The Crowbar is a tactical strike team of five questions that work in concert, each one setting up the next, cornering the core issues until there's nowhere left to hide. It's about strategic inquiry—the kind that requires Daniel and I to team up and tackle each challenge in sequence, knowing that skipping a step means missing a critical piece

Unearth Core Issues with The Crowbar

of the puzzle. It's like a combination lock; you need all five numbers, in the right order, to crack open the vault.

Understanding the Challenging Questions

The Crowbar is a systematic approach that digs deep, reaching into the bedrock of a business's true challenges and dreams. It's about using 5 probing questions that act as keys, opening doors to previously hidden rooms in the vast mansion of a client's experiences and strategies.

And here's a pro tip: lay out a table with the topics of each Crowbar question at the top of the columns, jot down the answers below, and watch as themes start to emerge across the board. If you do this right, it should feel like a brainstorming exercise where every answer that is said is also recorded. This type of visual will reveal patterns and connections, sharpening your focus on the issues that truly matter.

Here are the 5 questions, in the order I ask them.

"What are we doing right?"

Affirm Your Strengths: Beginning with "What are we doing right?" sets a foundation of positivity. It's a crucial step because it acknowledges the efforts and successes that exist, providing a balanced perspective. This question is invaluable because it builds confidence and reminds clients like Daniel that not all is lost; there are strengths to build upon.

Unearth Core Issues with The Crowbar

"What feels like it's not working?"

Identify Shortfalls: Transitioning to "What feels like it's not working?" shifts the focus to areas needing attention. This question is potent because it opens the door for clients to share their perceived failures, a necessary step for unearthing deeper issues. It provides a safe space for acknowledgement of challenges, which is the first step toward addressing them.

"What seems fuzzy right now?"

Clarify Uncertainty: Asking "What seems fuzzy right now?" targets the ambiguous areas of strategy or execution. Its utility lies in pinpointing where clarity and focus are needed, guiding the client to recognize areas of uncertainty that require some clarification or detail.

"What is not here, but should be?"

Recognize Absences: "What is not here, but should be?" invites clients to consider what essential elements might be missing from their strategy or operations. This question is a beacon, highlighting gaps that need to be filled for progress to begin. It's about uncovering the unseen, identifying what needs to be introduced or developed to move forward.

"What doesn't belong or doesn't fit?"

Eliminate Excess: Finally, "What doesn't belong or doesn't fit?" helps identify redundancies or misalignments. This inquiry is crucial for it assists in discerning what's hindering progress. It's about pruning the client's strategy of things that don't fit. Hopefully by removing what's stunting growth gives us the room to focus on the core issues. We are

Unearth Core Issues with The Crowbar

literally clearing the noise.

The Utility of These 5 Questions

The Crowbar technique digs deep, unearthing data but also providing direction. For Daniel, this meant zeroing in on the core problem plaguing his tech firm. It was a surgical strike to the heart of his company's woes. They highlighted the highs worth a toast, shed light on the glitches needing a fix, made blurry areas sharp, spotted the gaps in innovation, and chopped what needed to go. We rolled up our sleeves together—advisor and client, side by side—sifting through the answers to reveal the crux of the matter that once solved, paves the way for real growth and transformation.

The Outcome of The Crowbar

The Crowbar isn't just about asking the hard stuff—it's about the artful nudge towards revelation and growth. Think of it as the strategic chisel that chips away at the surface, revealing the bedrock truths beneath a client's business strategy. It's a deep dive beyond the numbers and plans, a dive that unearths the real issues, the hidden hurdles, and the gold nuggets of opportunity. This technique isn't for the faint-hearted; it's for the bold, the ones looking to forge real change and achieve lasting success. It's a powerful tool to find the hidden problems holding a business back and what can propel it forward.

Identifying and Addressing The Root Causes

The Crowbar is like detective work in the business world, uncovering clues that lead to the heart of the matter. Daniel's company? It needed more than a facelift; we needed to get to the bottom of what's been holding it back. With The Crowbar, we don't just spot the problems; we root them out, clear them up, and set the stage for solid, sustainable growth. It's about getting to the core, where the true transformation begins.

The Essence of Root Cause Analysis

Through a structured set of questions, The Crowbar method applies pressure where it's needed, prying open the tightly held defenses that guard the core issues. This is not an exercise in force but one of strategic leverage—using the right questions to apply just enough pressure to reveal what lies beneath.

The Impact of Deep Dive Analysis

This technique ensures that the process of identifying root causes isn't merely an academic exercise but a practical, actionable exploration. It's about constructing a blueprint for change, where each identified issue is matched with a strategy tailored to address it effectively.

Transforming Insights into Actions

The true knack of The Crowbar isn't just in the digging; it's in the doing. When we start prodding around with those five pointed questions, we're like detectives turning over clues. And more often than not, the answers point to causes we never even had on our radar, showing the real impact of issues we might've overlooked. Take, for instance, a small business struggling with cash flow. The Crowbar might reveal a common theme across the answers—a lack of strategy in  client payment terms, leading to a cash crunch. The insights gained aren't just eye-openers; they're actionable intel. It's about turning those 'Aha!' moments into 'Let's get on this' plans, transforming those roots of trouble into routes to success.

Let's take a look at how Daniel and I's conversation went.

Case Study: Breaking Through Denial

Caught in stagnation, Daniel's tech firm was spinning its wheels, unable to gain traction in an ever-evolving industry. Making things worse was Daniel's inability to describe the problem. He was all over the place and most of the things he talked about were emotional, not financial or strategic. I felt like he was just talking about the surface and shifting blame away from the real issue.

Unearth Core Issues with The Crowbar

The Interaction

I started off with a disarmingly simple yet profound question:

"What are we doing right?"

- "Our technology is cutting-edge, and our development team is incredibly talented."
- "We have a loyal customer base that believes in our products."
- "Our brand is well-recognized in the industry."

Daniel's company has some strong pillars holding it up. Their technology stands at the forefront of the industry, driven by a talented development team that's second to none. Customers are loyal, backing the brand with unwavering support. The company's brand itself is a well-recognized name in the tech world. These strengths form the foundation, but without addressing underlying issues, they may not be enough to sustain growth.

This one question set me up perfectly to being The Crowbar. I then drew the 5 columns on a white board, and just wrote down his answers as he gave them. Here were the results.

"What feels like it's not working?"

- "There's a significant communication gap between departments, leading to frequent misunderstandings."
- "We lack clear leadership and direction, which causes confusion and demotivation among employees."
- "Our decision-making process is slow, and we often miss market opportunities."

Unearth Core Issues with The Crowbar

When we look at what's broken, communication stands out as a major issue. Departments aren't talking to each other, leading to misunderstandings and missed connections. Leadership is another sore spot—there's no clear direction, which leaves employees feeling like they're drifting without a rudder. Decision-making is painfully slow, causing them to miss out on key market opportunities. These cracks in the foundation need fixing to prevent further stagnation.

"What seems fuzzy right now?"

- "Employees are unclear about their roles and responsibilities, leading to duplication of effort."
- "Our marketing strategy seems inconsistent, and we don't have a clear target audience."
- "There's a lot of uncertainty about the company's future direction and goals."

Confusion reigns supreme in Daniel's company. Employees are unsure about their roles, leading to duplicated efforts and wasted energy. The marketing strategy is all over the place, lacking consistency and a clear target audience. On top of that, there's a fog surrounding the company's future direction and goals, leaving everyone from top to bottom scratching their heads. Clearing up this confusion is crucial to steering the ship back on course.

"What is not here, but should be?"

- "We need a stronger vision and mission to guide our efforts and unite the team."
- "There's a lack of effective communication channels for feedback and ideas."
- "We don't have enough support for employee development and training."

Unearth Core Issues with The Crowbar

Daniel's company is missing a unifying vision and mission to rally the team. Effective communication channels are absent, stifling feedback and innovative ideas. Employee development and training are also lacking, which means the team isn't growing or evolving. By addressing these gaps, the company can build a more cohesive and forward-moving organization.

"What doesn't belong or doesn't fit?"

- "We have too many overlapping projects that dilute our focus and resources."
- "There's an excessive amount of bureaucracy that slows down our processes."
- "We're spending too much time on non-core activities that don't add value."

There's too much going on that's diluting the company's focus. Overlapping projects are pulling resources in different directions, causing inefficiencies. Bureaucracy is bogging down processes, making everything slower and more cumbersome. Additionally, the team is spending too much time on non-core activities that don't add real value. Streamlining efforts will help sharpen their competitive edge.

Common Theme

The BIG issue in Daniel's company is the lack of clear communication and leadership. Did you notice the words I bolded in his answers? In the real scenario, these were the words I circled on the table we created.

The communication and leadership issue is evident in the significant communication gap between departments and the absence of clear

Unearth Core Issues with The Crowbar

leadership and direction, as highlighted in **what's broken**. The confusion about roles and the company's future direction, mentioned in **what's confused**, further points to this theme. Additionally, the lack of effective communication channels and support for employee development in **what's missing** points to a deeper need for stronger, more cohesive leadership. Addressing these areas will be critical for turning things around and driving growth.

Action Plan for Daniel

When I sat down with Daniel, it became clear that his company's main issue is the lack of clear communication and leadership. Here's the homework I laid out for him to get things back on track:

1. **Establish a Clear Vision and Mission:** Define a strong, unifying vision and mission that everyone can rally behind.
2. **Improve Executive Alignment:** Conduct regular leadership meetings to ensure all executives are on the same page and communicating effectively.
3. **Implement Structured Communication Channels:** Set up clear communication channels across all departments to eliminate misunderstandings and enhance collaboration.
4. **Invest in Leadership Training:** Provide leadership training for managers to help them offer clear direction and support to their teams.
5. **Simplify Decision-Making Processes:** Streamline decision-making to be more agile and responsive to market opportunities.
6. **Prioritize Employee Development:** Create opportunities for employee development, feedback, and innovation to keep the team motivated and growing.

By focusing on these areas, Daniel can build a stronger, more unified team and drive his company forward. It's not a financial plan, but it impacts the financial statements. Just remember... Give this plan out in bite sized consumable chunks of information. You can show your client the whole plan, but only give them 1-3 things to work on between meetings.

The Comparison: A Path Not Taken

If I hadn't used The Crowbar technique during my conversation with Daniel, we would have stayed on the surface of his company's issues. Instead of diving into the root causes, Daniel would have continued to avoid the real problems. He'd likely keep investing time and resources in the wrong areas, driven by inertia rather than strategic insight. This approach would lead to further stagnation and potential decline for his firm, as the core issues would remain unaddressed.

Final Thoughts on Breaking Through Denial

In my experience, breaking through denial is one of the toughest but most crucial steps in addressing business issues. With Daniel, it was clear that his initial evasiveness was a barrier to progress. By employing The Crowbar technique, we were able to cut through the superficial layers and get to the heart of the matter. It's not easy for any leader to admit that their company has deep-rooted problems,

Unearth Core Issues with The Crowbar

especially when those issues might reflect on their own leadership. However, confronting these truths head-on is essential for growth and recovery. Daniel's willingness to face the uncomfortable realities of his business's challenges is the first step towards real change. By acknowledging the problems and taking decisive action, he can steer his company out of stagnation and onto a path of sustainable growth.

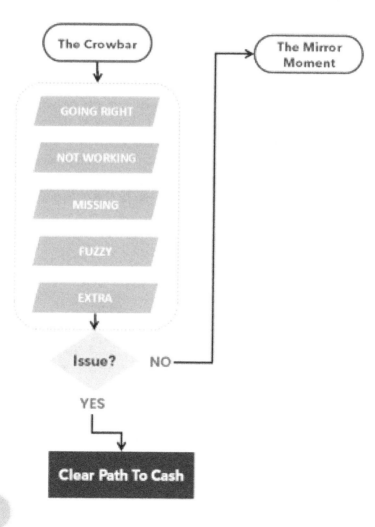

Chapter Six

REFLECTING FOR GROWTH

The Mirror Moment

Best Used When: the client isn't able to see the problem themselves, but they might be able to recognize similarities in another person's situation to their own.

E very business owner who has experienced real growth hits that critical spot—a 'Mirror Moment.' It's that clear-eyed standstill where you see the full picture, not just pieces. We're about to dive into The Mirror Moment technique. Think of it as more than a reality check; it's the push you need to align your daily grind with your big dream. This technique goes beyond just looking in the mirror. It's about recognizing your own issues reflected in the actions of others and setting a clear path to get where you want to be.

The Essence of Reflection

The Mirror Moment is more than a technique; it's a catalyst for profound behavioral adjustment. It holds up a metaphorical mirror, helping clients see themselves not just as they imagine, but as they truly are. This reflection includes their business operations, leadership styles, and daily decisions. It's about recognizing your own story in the actions of others, especially when you can't see

Reflecting for Growth The Mirror Moment

the problem or achievement yourself. This technique shines a light on the alignment—or misalignment—between your actions and your aspirations, driving a deeper sense of self-awareness and clarity.

Cultivating Self-Awareness

At the heart of this method is the encouragement of self-awareness. It's about taking a deliberate pause in the constant hustle, a moment to look back and see the trails you've blazed and the bridges you've burned. This introspection is crucial because understanding where you stand is the first step to mapping out where you need to go. Through reflective questioning, clients like Elena are prompted to consider not just the outcomes of their actions but the motivations and patterns that led to those results. This deeper insight helps chart a clearer path forward.

Accountability in Action

Reflection is just the beginning; real accountability comes from seeing yourself clearly in the story you're told and using that insight to drive change. The Mirror Moment isn't just about recognizing where you stand; it's about igniting the motivation to not just know better but to do better. It ensures that your daily hustle is aligned with your big-picture goals, turning every action into a deliberate step toward your ultimate vision.

The Story of Change

The story of Elena is a compelling illustration of The Mirror Moment in action. Elena had a driver personality, and it scared her employees. I could tell it immediately when I started working with her. Even though her boutique shop was struggling with inconsistent sales and just couldn't retain customers; the biggest issue was that Elena thought her style was just enforcing a standard, and that "tough love" is what got results in business. It was obvious that Elena saw her business' problems as the result of unproductive employees, not a leadership problem. This was the perfect time to use The Mirror Moment technique. So, I told Elena a story about another manager who was super direct when he talked to his employees.

This manager, much like Elena, believed that being tough was the only way to get things done. However, his approach created a tense work environment, leading to high turnover and low morale. When he finally saw himself through the eyes of his employees, he realized that his style was more about control than leadership. This revelation was his Mirror Moment. He understood that his behavior was driving people away, not inspiring them to perform better.

Elena saw herself in that story. It was a turning point. She realized that her "tough love" wasn't fostering a culture of accountability but one of fear. By reflecting on this, Elena recognized her role in the issues and committed to changing her approach. She started to communicate more openly, showing empathy and support, which transformed her team's dynamics and productivity.

The Mirror Moment isn't just about seeing where you stand; it's about understanding the impact of your actions and making deliberate changes to align your leadership style with your business goals. It's about recognizing that the deepest changes start with you, right there in the mirror's reflection. This self-awareness and accountability drive real progress, turning every action into a step toward your ultimate vision.

Encouraging Self-Awareness

Self-awareness is key in the game of business and personal growth. It's like putting on glasses that bring everything into sharp focus. The Mirror Moment steps up here as that clear lens, giving folks like Elena the chance to see their actions ripple out across the surface of their business pond.

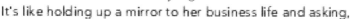

But kickstarting this process means talking about someone else's story first—someone who's not even in the room. By sharing a third-person tale that mirrors Elena's situation, it allows her to view her own world from the outside looking in, to spot what's really going on without the noise of self-judgment. It's like holding up a mirror to her business life and asking,

"See that story? What stands out for you here?"

The Power of Reflection for Self-Awareness

Self-awareness is a game-changer. It's the cornerstone of personal and professional growth. When you truly understand your strengths, weaknesses, and the impact of your actions, you can steer your path with purpose. The Mirror Moment lets you see the bigger picture and how your daily grind aligns with your ultimate goals. It's about recognizing the gaps and taking deliberate steps to bridge them. In business, this clarity turns challenges into opportunities and drives meaningful progress. When you're self-aware, every move is a calculated stride towards success.

How The Mirror Moment Encourages Self-Awareness and Accountability

"What stands out to you about that story?"

Illuminating Patterns: The Mirror Moment technique invites leaders to review their narratives, identifying recurring themes or behaviors. This is about recognition— spotting the patterns that serve as signposts on the journey of growth. It lays the groundwork for accountability by making leaders conscious of their impact on the business.

"Is there anything you would change if you saw this happening?"

Considering Alternatives: This question forces the individual to not only recognize these patterns but to consider if they can produce results. It's a prompt for your client to evaluate their current behavior and how it's helping them to achieve their goals.

"What would you do different in this situation?"

Strategic Adjustment: Transitioning from recognition to action, this inquiry encourages leaders to think proactively, to envision how they might realign their strategies with their goals based on this self-reflection. It holds your client accountable by asking them to commit to specific, actionable steps that address the identified issues. Best part of this step is that it comes from your client. They said it, so it must be true.

Reflecting for Growth The Mirror Moment

"Does this match what you are trying to do in your business?"

Aligning Behavior with Vision: Perhaps most crucially, this question serves as the linchpin of the technique, directly correlating the leader's actions with their long-term objectives. It's the moment of truth, where reflection meets reality, and the path forward begins to clear. It forces leaders to reckon with any misalignments and to take corrective action.

A Contrast to Unreflective Practices

When a business owner can't see the Issues, it's like driving with blinders on. They might keep pushing forward, thinking everything's fine, but in reality, they're heading straight for a cliff. Without recognizing the problems, they'll continue making the same mistakes, wasting time and resources on unproductive efforts. Employee morale can tank, leading to high turnover and a toxic work environment. The business stagnates, unable to adapt or grow, because the leader is stuck in a cycle of denial.

Ignoring issues doesn't just stall progress; it sets the stage for decline. Customers start to notice the cracks and lose confidence, competitors seize the opportunity to pull ahead, and before long, the once-thriving business is struggling to stay afloat. But it doesn't have to be this way. By facing the hard truths and becoming self-aware, a business owner can turn things around, transforming challenges into steppingstones for success.

The Outcome of Self Awareness

Using The Mirror Moment technique is like stepping into a ring with your true self—it's raw, it's real, and it's about mustering the guts to

Reflecting for Growth The Mirror Moment

face the music. This isn't your everyday self-scrutiny; it's deep diving into what makes your business tick, or what's throwing a wrench in the works. By reflecting on what you're doing, why you're doing it, and how it matches up with where you wanna go, you're not just checking yourself, you're steering the ship right. This isn't about ego, it's about getting your business groove back on track—spotting your wins, nosing out the snags, and syncing your daily grind with your big dream blueprint. Your role as an advisor is to help them make their dream happen. You are in the dream fulfillment business!

94

94

Reflecting for Growth The Mirror Moment

Case Study: A Client's Moment of Clarity

Let me tell you about Elena and her boutique. On the surface, it was a stylish success, but underneath, there were real issues—sales were all over the place, and customers weren't coming back. Elena thought it was because her employees weren't performing. She believed her tough love approach was the way to get results. It was clear she needed a Mirror Moment.

The Interaction

One morning, I told Elena a story about another manager who was just like her—direct and tough on his team.

"What would you do to turn their situation around?" I asked her.

As she started thinking it through, she mentioned open communication and valuing each team member's voice. I pushed further,

"And what if the leadership style itself was the problem?"

As Elena thought about solutions for this other business, a light bulb went off.

"How do these ideas apply to your team?" I asked.

That question hit home. She realized her tough approach was causing more harm than good.

The Purpose of Each Question

"What would you do to turn their situation around?"

Reflection on Feedback: I wanted Elena to see things from her team's perspective, to understand their experiences.

"And what if the leadership style itself was the problem?"

Recognition of Patterns: I helped her connect the dots between her leadership style and the problems her business was facing.

"How do these ideas apply to your team?"

Call to Action: I pushed her to think about changes she needed to make and to start planning those changes.

"Does this match what you are trying to do in your business?"

Alignment with Vision: I made sure she understood that her day-to-day actions needed to match her bigger goals.

The Impact of The Mirror Moment

Elena's realization was huge. She saw that her tough love approach was out of sync with her vision for the business. She jumped into action, getting involved with her team, holding regular training sessions, and really listening to her employees. Her "customer-first" motto became a real practice, not just a slogan on the wall.

Reflecting for Growth The Mirror Moment

A Contrast to Unreflective Leadership

Now, picture if I hadn't walked Elena through The Mirror Moment. She'd probably still be blaming her employees, missing the real issue. Sales would keep dropping, and customers wouldn't come back. Without self-awareness and action, those problems would have just gotten worse.

Final Thoughts on The Moments of Clarity

Achieving moments of self-awareness is difficult and essential for business growth. With Elena, her tough love approach was more harmful than helpful. The Mirror Moment helped us peel back the layers and get to the core of the issue.

It's challenging for any leader to realize that their management style might be the problem. However, this realization is essential for true progress. Elena's willingness to see herself in the story I shared and to face the realities of her leadership was the first step toward meaningful change. By acknowledging her role in the issues and taking decisive action, she transformed her team dynamics and set her business on a path to sustainable growth.

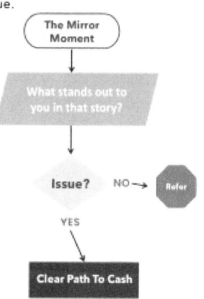

Cash Flow Mike

Part-3
Elevate:

Advancing
Towards Goals

98

Now that we've dug deep and uncovered the core issues, it's time to shift gears. In Part III, "Elevate - Advancing Toward Goals," we take those insights and turn them into action. This phase is all about building momentum and driving forward. We use the clarity and understanding we've gained to propel our clients toward achieving their visions. It's about taking those hard-earned insights and transforming them into real, tangible results. This is where we turn breakthroughs into steppingstones for future success, amplifying every achievement and pushing toward the next goal.

The Economic Echo Technique

Alright, let's cut to the chase with the Economic Echo. It's like this: every choice you make in business, every dollar you spend or don't, it's gonna circle back to you. This technique's all about cranking up the volume on what those financial moves are really saying. It ain't just about what's happening right now; it's about the big picture, the long haul. We use the cold, hard numbers to give you the full scoop on where you're at and where you're heading. It's all about making moves that count, lining up those actions so that every play you make builds up your cash flow and sets you up for the win.

The Economic Echo isn't just about crunching numbers; it's about translating them into a clear strategy for growth. We take the abstract and make it tangible, turning graphs and spreadsheets into a compass that guides clients through the maze of financial decisions. This approach helps them navigate towards profitability and sustainability. It's all about using the data to create a roadmap for success, making every financial choice a step in the right direction.

The Accolade Anchor Technique

Then, we celebrate with The Accolade Anchor, a technique that recognizes the journey's milestones and the victories along the way. It's an acknowledgment that every success, no matter its scale, is a testament to progress, perseverance, and potential. This method is about more than applause; it's about anchoring our clients in a state of motivation and confidence, using the glow of past achievements to light the way for future endeavors.

The Accolade Anchor turns success into a solid foundation and a launchpad for even greater achievements. It's a reminder that each victory is not just an endpoint but a milestone on a continuous journey of growth. This technique ensures that celebrating success isn't the finish line—it's the starting point for setting new goals and dreaming bigger. It's all about using those wins to fuel the fire for the next big leap.

The Elevation Sequence: A Symphony of Strategic Interactions

The Elevation Sequence is more than a set of techniques—it's a holistic approach that elevates client conversations and their financial narratives. This sequence takes you from understanding to action, from reflection to celebration. Each step is deliberate, each technique a crucial note in a greater symphony of strategic interaction that empowers clients to deeply engage with their financial journeys and elevate their stories of success.

As we explore these techniques, we act as co-navigators and cheerleaders, guiding clients through the waters of financial decision-making and championing their aspirations. Part III is about moving forward, leveraging the insights and strengths uncovered in our journey to chart a course towards goals that once seemed distant but now, with clarity, confidence, and a celebration of achievements, are well within reach.

In "Elevate - Advancing Toward Goals," the focus shifts to turning dreams and aspirations into living, breathing realities. We set our sights on the stars, helping clients achieve what once seemed impossible.

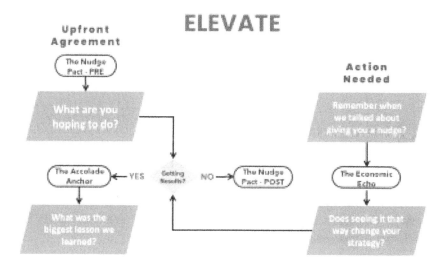

Chapter Seven

UNDERSTANDING FINANCIAL IMPACT
The Economic Echo

Best Used When: you are wanting to connect an action your client needs to take in order to improve their financial situation.

Here's the deal with the Economic Echo: think of your business decisions like a series of dominoes. You tip one, and they all start falling into place, creating an echo that reverberates through your company's future. This isn't just about the dollars you're counting today; it's about making sure those dominoes are set up to fall perfectly tomorrow, next year, and beyond.

In Chapter 7, "The Economic Echo: Understanding Financial Impact," we dig into how your financial actions create ripples. We'll explore strategies that make every decision count, aligning your cash moves with your long-term goals. It's about seeing how small actions today echo back in the form of dollars, growing your business and boosting your bottom line. We're turning up the volume on decision-making, ensuring that when you make a move, your future answers back with the sound of success.

The Resonance of Financial Decisions

The Economic Echo technique is all about making smart decisions that pay off. Think of it as financial foresight; every choice you make today will echo back in the form of dollars tomorrow. With this technique, we help clients like Owen see how their financial moves today will impact their business's profitability down the line. It's practical and direct, turning insights into actions that resonate with success.

Amplifying Insights into Action

The Economic Echo is all about translating financial data into a strategy. It involves a series of carefully crafted questions that highlight the tangible outcomes of financial strategies. These questions aren't just prompts; they spark deeper understanding and strategic planning. They push clients to engage actively with their financial data, seeing beyond the numbers to grasp the stories those numbers tell about efficiency, growth potential, and areas ripe for innovation.

Financial Data as a Strategic Compass

Through The Economic Echo, financial data becomes a compass, guiding businesses towards informed decisions and strategic adjustments. This technique empowers business owners to navigate their operations with confidence, using insights to steer toward profitability and away from pitfalls. It's about spotting financial trends that signal opportunities, uncovering inefficiencies that hurt profitability, and recognizing the strengths that can drive future success.

The Story of Transformation

Owen's story sheds light on how The Economic Echo technique takes the guesswork out of financial planning. When Owen's coffee shops hit a wall—sales up, profits flat—I knew it was time to echo things out. We sifted through the numbers, not just for a quick fix but to understand and act on the underlying issues. The breakthrough came when Owen's numbers told a story he hadn't heard before, one where he could steer his ship towards greater profits. It's a journey from financial fog to clear-cut strategy, with every dollar and decision pointing the way forward.

The Economic Echo: A Symphony of Strategy

This chapter promises to unfold The Economic Echo technique in all its depth and breadth. It's an exploration of how financial data, when properly interpreted and acted upon, can resonate through every aspect of a business, creating a harmonious alignment between daily operations and long-term objectives. Through The Economic Echo, we transform financial data from static numbers into dynamic narratives of strategic development, profitability, and growth. The financial impact or echo is the reason the action needs to be taken. It's the reward!

Understanding Financial Impact The Economic Echo

Interpreting Financial Data for Strategic Decisions

When it comes down to brass tacks in business, it's not just about the numbers—it's about what they're telling you. The Economic Echo technique focuses on understanding the story behind the numbers. It's like having a conversation with your business's past and future, all through the lens of your ledger. This chapter peels back the curtain on this technique, showing you how to turn those dry figures into a game plan that'll take your business from where it's at to where you've dreamed it could be.

The Economic Echo: Amplifying Financial Insight

Advisors, this one's important. The Economic Echo is all about cause and effect—plain and simple. You advise, they act, and the results echo back in their financials. Show your clients how every decision has a financial echo, and that echo tells them whether they're on track or off course. It's about making sure they see the connection between today's choices and tomorrow's bottom line. Teach them to look for the echo—because when they make the right moves, they'll see the benefits ringing clear in their cash flow.

The Utility of Financial Data Interpretation

Understanding financial data is pivotal for several reasons:

- **Strategic Alignment:** It ensures that every financial decision is aligned with the company's broader strategic goals. This alignment is critical for maintaining a coherent direction towards growth and profitability.

- **Resource Optimization:** By interpreting financial data, businesses can identify areas where resources are either underutilized or overstretched, allowing for adjustments that optimize operational efficiency.

- **Risk Mitigation:** Insightful interpretation of financial data helps in identifying potential risks before they escalate, enabling preemptive measures to safeguard the company's assets and future.

- **Innovation and Growth:** Financial data often hold the keys to unlocking new opportunities for innovation and expansion. Proper interpretation can reveal patterns and trends that point towards unexplored avenues for growth.

Implementing The Economic Echo

The implementation of The Economic Echo technique involves several key questions and actions:

"Based on this financial data, what should we do next?"

This question compels business leaders to view data not just as historical records but as signposts for future action. It encourages a forward-looking perspective, where data-driven insights form the basis of strategic planning.

"Does seeing the numbers like this change the way you think about what you're doing?"

This question challenges leaders to reassess their current strategies in a new way. It fosters adaptability, urging a reconsideration of approaches based on solid financial evidence.

"Based on this snapshot, what stands out to you?"

Here, the focus is on immediate, striking insights that emerge from financial data. It's about identifying anomalies, trends, or results that demand attention and potentially, action.

"Can you identify any financial trends that point towards an opportunity for action?"

This encourages a deeper analysis, looking beyond the present to understand financial trajectories and their implications for the business's future.

From Data to Action:
The Economic Echo in Practice

In Owen's case, The Economic Echo technique really shines. Owen was scratching his head over his rising sales that weren't translating into higher profits. That's where I stepped in with The Economic Echo, turning those confusing numbers into a strategy session. It wasn't just about spotting problems; it was about pinpointing solutions that hit the mark—like streamlining how Owen got his goods, tweaking his prices, or doubling down on what's selling like hotcakes. This approach turned his financial data into a clear game plan, paving the way for real growth and profitability.

A Contrast: The Path Not Taken

Without using The Economic Echo to guide financial decisions, business owners are essentially flying blind. They might see numbers on a balance sheet, but they miss the story behind them. This can lead to missed opportunities, inefficient spending, and decisions that don't align with long-term goals. Without this technique, it's easy to overlook areas that need improvement or potential growth. The result? Stagnant profits, wasted resources, and a business that struggles to move forward. The Economic Echo turns raw data into actionable insights, and ignoring it means missing out on a clear path to success.

Case Study: From Data to Action

Owen's coffee shops were known for their quality and innovation. Despite rising sales, profits weren't following suit. That's when I stepped in with The Economic Echo technique to clear up the confusion.

The Interaction

I sat down with Owen, handed him the financials, and asked,

"Based on this financial data, what should we do next?"

This got Owen thinking about strategic actions rather than just numbers.

Understanding Financial Impact The Economic Echo

Owens response:

- *"I think we need to look at our supply chain and see if there are any cost-saving opportunities."*
- *"Maybe we should focus on marketing our best-selling products more aggressively."*
- *"We might need to adjust our pricing strategy to improve our profit margins."*

As we dug deeper, I asked,

"Does seeing the numbers like this change the way you think about your strategy?"

This made Owen reflect on his current operations and how they lined up with the financial health of his shops.

Owen's response:

- *"Yes, I didn't realize how much we were spending on certain supplies. We need to find more cost-effective options."*
- *"It's clear now that some of our efforts aren't yielding the expected returns. We should pivot to more profitable initiatives."*
- *"I see that our overhead costs are higher than I thought. We need to streamline operations."*

"Based on this snapshot, what stands out to you?"

I continued, helping Owen identify the most urgent issues in the financial data.

Owen's response:

- "Our labor costs seem to be eating into our profits more than I anticipated."
- "The sales for our seasonal products are great, but they're not translating into overall profitability."
- "I noticed that our online sales are increasing, but our in-store sales are stagnant."

Finally, I asked,

"Can you identify any financial trends that point towards an opportunity for action?"

This encouraged Owen to look ahead and plan based on the trends he saw.

Owen's response:

- "It looks like our weekend sales are significantly higher. Maybe we should run promotions during the week to balance it out."
- "The data shows that our loyalty program members spend more. We should invest in expanding that program."
- "Our new product lines are performing well. We should consider expanding those offerings."

The Purpose and Utility of Each Question

"What should we do next?" got Owen actively involved in planning, moving him from a passive observer to an active participant.

"Does seeing the numbers like this change the way you think about your strategy?" challenged Owen's existing views and highlighted the need to align operations with financial realities.

"What stands out to you?" helped Owen focus on the most critical issues, prioritizing where to take action first.

"Can you identify any financial trends that point towards an opportunity for action?" pushed Owen to think strategically about the future, turning insights into actionable plans.

From Data to Action: The Transformation

With a clear focus, Owen took action. He addressed inefficiencies in his supply chain and found more cost-effective options. He also boosted marketing for his best-selling products and expanded the loyalty program. Additionally, he adjusted his pricing strategy and streamlined operations to reduce overhead costs. These moves, guided by The Economic Echo, not only improved profitability but set up his business for long-term growth.

A Contrast: The Path Not Taken

If Owen had ignored The Economic Echo, he might have kept wasting resources on unprofitable areas and missed out on growth opportunities. This lack of insight could have led to declining profits and possibly the end of his business.

Final Thoughts on From Data to Action

The case study of Owen highlights the profound impact of the Economic Echo technique in turning financial data into strategic action. Through a series of targeted questions, Owen moved from confusion to clarity, making informed decisions that boosted his business's profitability and growth.

This journey underscores the importance of not just understanding financial data but using it as a springboard for strategic decision-making. The Economic Echo technique shows how powerful financial insights can be when harnessed correctly, offering a clear roadmap for businesses to navigate the complex interplay between financial health and strategic success. It's about transforming numbers into actionable plans, ensuring every decision is data-driven and geared towards long-term growth.

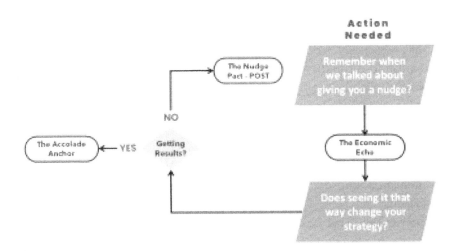

Chapter Eight

CELEBRATING SUCCESS
The Accolade Anchor

Best Used When: taking a moment to celebrate a win or when you are wanting to motivate your client into take the next step toward another achievement.

A s we move into Part III, "Elevate - Advancing Toward Goals," we come to a technique that's both simple and powerful—the Accolade Anchor. This chapter explores how celebrating successes can pave the way for future achievements. It's about recognizing victories, big and small, as vital moments that drive growth, innovation, and motivation. Celebrating these wins isn't just about patting yourself on the back; it's about using them as steppingstones for continued progress and reaching new heights.

The Essence of Celebration in Growth

Celebration is a powerful tool for growth. Recognizing and celebrating victories, no matter how small, fuels motivation and drives innovation. It's about building momentum. When you take the time to acknowledge achievements, you reinforce what's working and set a positive tone for the future. These moments of recognition create a culture of success, keeping everyone focused and energized. In essence, celebrating wins turns

113

progress into a habit, propelling your business toward continuous growth and new milestones.

Transforming Success into Strategy

The Accolade Anchor isn't just about celebrating success—it's about using that success to inspire future achievements. Reaching a goal is a win, but the real power lies in how it fuels the next steps. This technique leverages the momentum from past achievements to drive forward, turning the thrill of success into a launchpad for new goals. It's about keeping the energy high and the progress steady, using each victory as a springboard for the journey ahead.

The Strategic Framework of the Accolade Anchor

The Accolade Anchor technique breaks down each success through a series of simple yet powerful reflections. It's as easy as saying, "Remember when..."

Recognizing Strengths: Start by identifying the strengths behind each victory. What personal and organizational capabilities led to success? This step highlights what's working well.

Reliving the Achievement: Take a moment to revisit the emotions and experiences of that success. This deepens the connection to those moments and reinforces the motivation to aim higher.

Building Upon Success: Use each achievement as a steppingstone for future goals. The Accolade Anchor promotes a mindset of continuous improvement and growth.

Learning from the Journey: Every success story has lessons to offer.

Celebrating Success The Accolade Anchor

This technique ensures that the wisdom gained from each victory is used to enhance future strategies and actions.

This strategic framework helps turn every win into a launchpad for even greater achievements, keeping the momentum going and the focus on continuous progress.

The Story of Empowerment: Clara's Victory

Let me tell you about Clara, a tech startup CEO who overcame a string of rejections to finally secure significant funding. This story shows the transformative power of the Accolade Anchor It's not just about celebrating success but dissecting it, understanding it, and using it to build confidence, clarity, and direction.

Chapter 8, "Accolade Anchor: Celebrating Successes," is all about the might of a well-earned high-five. It's about turning those wins into waypoints on your business map. This chapter is about loading your arsenal with the power of past victories to catapult you to new heights. It's a nod to every win, big or small, reminding us that our path is lined with lessons learned and fueled by the drive that got us over previous hurdles. By spotlighting these wins, we're not just reminiscing; we're reloading for the next leap forward.

Recognizing Achievements

Recognizing achievements is both a compass and an anchor in the journey toward personal and professional development. It guides individuals through doubt and anchors them in confidence and clarity. The Accolade Anchor technique focuses on celebrating successes, using past victories to light the way forward. This section explores the importance of recognizing achievements as a crucial strategy for sustained growth and motivation, rather than just a pat on the back. Leveraging every win keeps you pushing toward your next goal.

The Essence of Celebrating Successes

At the heart of the Accolade Anchor technique is the belief that every achievement, whether big or small, shows resilience, capability, and progress. It's about creating memorable markers of success that serve as testimonials of past efforts and foundational stones for future goals. Recognizing achievements is crucial because it boosts motivation, reinforces what works, and sets the stage for even greater accomplishments.

Implementing the Accolade Anchor

The Accolade Anchor technique employs a series of reflective questions and actions designed to maximize the impact of recognizing achievements:

 "Let's look at (insert recent win),... what does that say about your strengths?"

Celebrating Success The Accolade Anchor

- **Identifying Strengths Through Success:** Asking, "Let's look at a recent win," pushes individuals to think about the skills and strategies that led to their success. This reflection helps understand what worked, enabling them to replicate and refine those elements in future efforts. It's a process of learning and improvement, not just celebration.

"How did it feel when you did that?"

- **Reliving Positive Emotions:** Asking, "How did it feel when you achieved that?" rekindles the positive emotions tied to success—joy, pride, satisfaction. This emotional reconnection makes you feel good and acts as a psychological reward, reinforcing the drive to pursue and achieve more goals.

"How can we use this going forward?"

- **Building on Success for Future Goals:** Asking, "How can we use this going forward?" shifts the focus from past wins to future goals. It's about using the momentum of current successes to push towards new targets. This question embodies the essence of the Accolade Anchor, turning each victory into a springboard for continued growth.

"What was the biggest lesson we learned then?"

- **Extracting Lessons from the Journey:** Asking, "What was the biggest lesson we learned?" ensures that every success is celebrated and examined for insights. This approach fosters a mindset of continuous learning, mining each achievement for valuable lessons that can enhance future strategies. It's about understanding what worked and applying that knowledge to keep improving and growing.

The Transformative Power of Recognition

The Accolade Anchor technique highlights the transformative power of recognition. When you take the time to celebrate achievements, you do more than just acknowledge a job well done—you create a powerful catalyst for future growth. Recognizing success boosts morale, reinforces effective strategies, and builds a culture of continuous improvement.

By identifying what led to each victory, you gain valuable insights that can be replicated and refined. This turns each success into a learning experience, providing a roadmap for future endeavors. It also strengthens the connection to your goals, making the journey ahead clearer and more focused.

Moreover, the Accolade Anchor encourages a forward-thinking mindset. By reflecting on past wins and asking key questions about how to leverage them, you set the stage for ongoing progress. This technique transforms recognition from a simple pat on the back into a strategic tool that drives sustained motivation and achievement.

In essence, the Accolade Anchor doesn't just celebrate success—it uses it as a springboard for even greater accomplishments, ensuring that each win propels you further along the path to your ultimate goals.

Celebrating Success The Accolade Anchor

Using Success as a Springboard for Future Goals

Celebrating success isn't just about acknowledgment; it's about using each win as a springboard for future goals. The Accolade Anchor technique leverages past victories to fuel forward momentum, intertwining recognition with progression. Every achievement, big or small, is a steppingstone that propels us toward the next goal.

The Strategic Lever of Success

Success is more than an outcome; it's a tool for future growth. Each win, whether a major deal or a small improvement, provides valuable lessons. By recognizing and studying these achievements, we build a playbook for future strategies. These victories fuel our progress, guiding us from one success to the next.

Building Momentum

The Accolade Anchor emphasizes the importance of momentum. Celebrating successes transforms potential stagnation into dynamic movement. Quick wins build on themselves, creating a positive cycle that drives individuals and organizations forward.

Cultivating a Culture of Achievement

Using success as a springboard fosters a culture of continuous improvement. Each achievement builds on the last, creating an upward spiral of growth. This culture values goal-oriented action and sets the stage for future victories.

The Mechanism of Springboarding Success

Leveraging success for future goals involves key steps:

- **Reflection and Recognition:** Start by reflecting on successes and recognizing the factors behind them. This practice helps identify strengths and strategies to replicate.

- **Emotional Reinvestment:** Positive emotions from success provide the motivation for pursuing new goals. They turn the memory of success into a renewable source of drive.

- **Strategic Analysis and Planning:** Analyze each success to understand how it was achieved. Use these insights to set SMART goals inspired by past achievements.

- **Lesson Integration and Forward Projection:** Integrate lessons from past successes into future strategies, ensuring goals are grounded in reality and aligned with previous achievements.

The Transformational Impact of Springboarding Success

Using success as a springboard transforms achievements from isolated events into interconnected chapters of continuous growth. The Accolade Anchor technique makes celebration a strategic tool for sustainable growth. Each success, no matter how small, propels us toward the next objective. It turns the act of celebration into

a launching pad for the future, driving individuals and organizations forward with confidence and momentum.

Case Study: The Power of Positive Reinforcement

Clara, the CEO of a growing tech startup, was at a critical point. After several rejections, her company finally secured significant funding. This win marked both an end and a beginning. Clara sought my help to ensure this success was celebrated and used as a catalyst for future victories.

The Interaction

I started our debrief by focusing on the strengths revealed by Clara's funding win.

"Let's look at your funding win, what does that say about you and your strengths as a leader and innovator?" I asked.

Responses from Clara:

- "It shows that my persistence and resilience paid off."
- "It highlights my ability to adapt our pitch based on feedback."
- "It demonstrates our team's innovative approach to solving industry problems."

As we talked, I explored the emotional landscape of Clara's achievement.

Celebrating Success The Accolade Anchor

"How did it feel when you finally did it?"

This allowed Clara to reconnect with the positive emotions tied to her success, boosting her morale and motivation to pursue further goals.

Responses from Clara:

- *"I felt an immense sense of relief and validation."*
- *"It was incredibly rewarding to see our hard work pay off."*
- *"I felt more confident in our vision and strategy."*

Looking ahead, I asked,

"How can we use this going forward?"

This question strategically steered Clara toward leveraging her recent success as a springboard for future objectives, emphasizing the Accolade Anchor's principle of building upon victories.

Responses from Clara:

- *"We can use this momentum to attract additional investors."*
- *"This success can boost our team's morale and drive future projects."*
- *"We should capitalize on this credibility to expand our market reach."*

Lastly, I sought to extract valuable insights from the journey.

"What was the biggest lesson we learned?"

I asked, encouraging Clara to distill her experience into actionable guide points for her startup's future strategies.

Celebrating Success The Accolade Anchor

Responses from Clara:

- *"I learned the importance of being adaptable and responsive to feedback."*
- *"Persistence is key, even in the face of multiple rejections."*
- *"Building strong relationships with potential investors is crucial."*

Why Each Question Was Asked

- **Recognizing Strengths:** My first question aimed to solidify Clara's understanding of her capabilities, ensuring her recent win translated into lasting confidence in her leadership and innovation skills.

- **Reflecting on Positive Emotions:** This question deepened Clara's emotional connection to her achievement, reinforcing the intrinsic motivation derived from success and the drive to continue her company's growth.

- **Foundation for Future Goals:** By prompting Clara to consider her success as a steppingstone, I facilitated a forward-looking mindset, encouraging strategic planning informed by proven strengths and recent wins.

- **Extraction of Lessons:** This inquiry was pivotal in transitioning from celebration to reflection, ensuring Clara and her team could learn from their experiences, enhancing their strategic approach moving forward.

The Impact of Positive Reinforcement

Through applying the Accolade Anchor technique, Clara not only celebrated her funding milestone but also emerged with a reinforced sense of confidence, a deeper connection to her success, and a strategic plan for leveraging this victory for her company's next set of goals. Energized by her newfound insights and the positive reinforcement of her achievements, Clara led her team to double their user base, illustrating the potent impact of acknowledging success as both an end and a means to further achievements.

A Contrast: The Path Not Taken

Imagine if Clara's success was merely noted without deeper reflection or strategic application. In this scenario, Clara misses the opportunity to solidify her confidence, understand the full extent of her strengths, and strategically harness the momentum of her success. Without the Accolade Anchor technique, this could lead to a fleeting sense of accomplishment, with Clara potentially reverting to old strategies without benefiting from the confidence and insights gained from her achievement.

Final Thoughts on Positive Reinforcement

The story of Clara shows how the Accolade Anchor technique goes beyond traditional celebrations of success. By recognizing achievements, reflecting on the journey, and planning strategically for the future, this approach turns victories into valuable assets for continued growth. It shows that with the right questions and reflective practices, each success becomes a powerful springboard, driving individuals and organizations toward their goals with renewed confidence, motivation, and clarity.

Celebrating Success The Accolade Anchor

In the future, we can recall the feeling from this success with a simple, "Remember when we..." This makes it easy to tap into the motivation and insights from past wins to fuel future achievements.

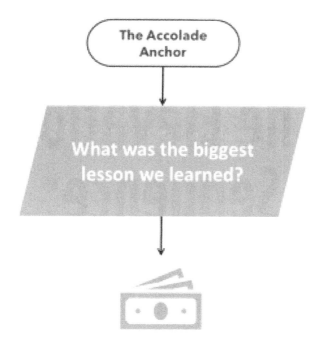

125

Cash Flow Mike

The Elevation Sequence:

Connecting Strategic Conversations To Actions

Cash Flow Mike

The Elevation Sequence is a game-changer for financial advising. It puts clients in control, recognizing that nobody likes to be told what to do. This approach quickly identifies issues in the company and categorizes them effectively. Whether it's about education, profit, cash flow, debt, operations, or future planning, The Elevation Sequence covers it all.

A Holistic Approach to Financial Advising

Throughout this journey, we've explored how each technique in The Elevation Sequence serves a unique purpose, from building trust to celebrating achievements. It's a comprehensive method that elevates advisor-client interactions beyond mere data exchange. Here's a quick recap of each technique:

- **The Compass Technique:** Establishes trust and aligns financial actions with client goals.
- **The Nudge Pact:** Motivates clients through a partnership, turning "I should" into "I will."
- **Clear The Noise:** Focuses on essentials by cutting through distractions.
- **The Explorer:** Uncovers hidden motivations and fears.
- **The Crowbar:** Applies strategic pressure to address core financial issues.
- **The Mirror Moment:** Encourages self-awareness and accountability.
- **The Economic Echo:** Amplifies the impact of financial decisions.
- **The Accolade Anchor:** Celebrates milestones and uses them as motivation for future success.

CashFlowMike

By integrating these methods, we create a richer, more meaningful advisory experience. Clients not only gain clarity and confidence but also engage deeply with their financial journey.

Client Control and Issue Identification

The strength of The Elevation Sequence lies in its ability to empower clients. Instead of dictating actions, it facilitates a process where clients take charge of their financial journey. By identifying issues in a structured way, clients gain a clear understanding of their challenges and the paths to overcome them. Here's how we break it down:

1. **Education** - Clients want to understand what they are looking at.

   - **Techniques:** The Home Run Financial System or The Financial Doctor
   - **Questions:**
     - *"Do you need a better understanding of your financial statements?"*
     - *"Are you looking to analyze your financial health like a doctor examines a patient?"*

2. **Profit** - The business isn't making money.

   - **Techniques:** Mining Your Business For Hidden Cash or Pricing and Cost Analysis
   - **Questions:**
     - *"Do you know where your hidden profits are?"*
     - *"Are you aware of how your pricing affects your bottom line?"*

CashFlowMike

3. **Cash Flow** - Clients never seem to have any money.

- **Techniques:** The Fast Money Formula or Mining Your Business For Hidden Cash
- **Questions:**
  - *"Are you struggling to keep cash flowing smoothly?"*
  - *"Do you need to uncover hidden cash within your business?"*

4. **Debt** - Clients are trying to acquire a loan or manage existing debt.

- **Techniques:** The Home Run Financial System (long term debt), The Fast Money Formula (short term debt), or How to Deal with Your Banker
- **Questions:**
  - *"Are you managing long-term debt effectively?"*
  - *"Do you need strategies to handle short-term debt?"*
  - *"Are you looking for better ways to negotiate with your banker?"*

5. **Operations** - There are issues with the business model or its execution.

- **Techniques:** Pricing calculators to validate business model or process diagramming of the issue
- **Questions:**
  - *"Is your business model yielding the desired results?"*
  - *"Do you need to map out your processes to identify bottlenecks?"*

6. **Future** - Clients are thinking about selling or exiting the business.

- **Techniques:** Start With The End In Mind, Forecasting By The

CashFlowMike

- Numbers, Simple Valuation Formula, and The Deliberate Exit Strategy
- Questions:
    - *"Are you planning for the future of your business?"*
    - *"Do you need to forecast and value your business for a potential exit?"*

For more information on The Clear Path To Cash Course, check out the book "Don't Be A D.U.M.B. Business Owner" by Cash Flow Mike or visit www.cashflowmike.com.

Connecting It All to "Don't Tell Me What To Do"

The title of the book, "Don't Tell Me What To Do," encapsulates the spirit of The Elevation Sequence. This approach is all about empowering clients, not dictating their actions. By using these techniques, advisors can guide clients to take ownership of their financial decisions. Here's how this philosophy is woven throughout The Elevation Sequence:

- Client Empowerment: Each technique is designed to put the client in control. From The Compass Technique, which builds trust and alignment, to The Accolade Anchor, which celebrates client achievements, every step ensures clients are the ones steering their financial journey.

- Issue Identification and Solutions: By quickly identifying the client's issues and categorizing them, advisors can tailor their approach to meet the client's specific needs. This ensures that clients feel heard and understood, rather than being told what to do.

Cash Flow Mike

- **Strategic Questions:** The use of strategic questions in each technique allows clients to reflect on their situation and come up with their own solutions. This fosters a sense of ownership and responsibility, as clients are actively involved in the decision-making process.

- **Building Confidence and Clarity:** Through techniques like The Mirror Moment and The Economic Echo, clients gain a deeper understanding of their financial habits and the impact of their decisions. This clarity empowers them to make informed choices, reinforcing the idea that they are in control of their financial future.

The Elevation Sequence is more than just a series of techniques; it's a strategic framework that transforms financial advising. By integrating these methods, advisors create a richer, more meaningful advisory experience. Clients not only gain clarity and confidence but also engage deeply with their financial journey. This approach aligns perfectly with the ethos of "Don't Tell Me What To Do," ensuring clients are empowered to take charge of their financial success.

Don't just TELL - transform. The Elevation Sequence is your blueprint for truly impactful conversations where you talk less and listen more - remember, 70% client, 30% advisor. That's the secret to ditching the lecture we tend to give our clients. Every question you ask, every technique you apply, is a deliberate step toward turning your clients' financial dreams into solid achievements. By sticking to this game plan, you'll build deeper relationships, spur clients to action, and lift their financial stories to new heights. Just remember to:

TERMINATE EVERY LONG LECTURE.

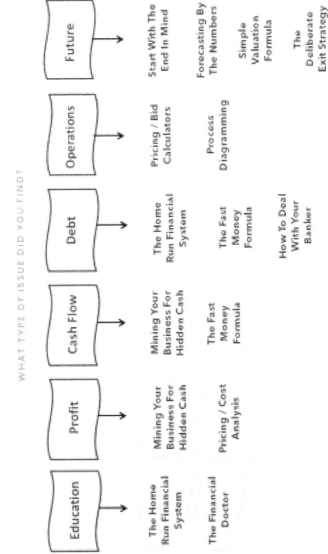

Cash Flow Mike

Clear PATH To Cash

WHAT TYPE OF ISSUE DID YOU FIND?

Education	Profit	Cash Flow	Debt	Operations	Future
The Home Run Financial System	Mining Your Business For Hidden Cash	Mining Your Business For Hidden Cash	The Home Run Financial System	Pricing / Bid Calculators	Start With The End In Mind
The Financial Doctor	Pricing / Cost Analysis	The Fast Money Formula	The Fast Money Formula	Process Diagramming	Forecasting By The Numbers
			How To Deal With Your Banker		Simple Valuation Formula
					The Deliberate Exit Strategy

ANALYZE, DIAGNOSE & TREAT - CREATE YOUR ACTION PLAN

Final Words

As we wrap up our journey through The Elevation Sequence, let's take a moment to reflect. If you've made it this far, kudos—you've braved the twists, turns, and occasional financial jargon without tossing this book into the nearest financial abyss. That's no small feat, and I salute you.

This book wasn't just meant to be a guide but a companion in the often turbulent voyage of financial planning. From establishing trust and understanding with The Compass Technique to celebrating achievements with The Accolade Anchor, we've covered a lot of ground. If there's one thing I hope you remember, it's this: financial planning isn't a spectator sport. It's a dance—a sometimes awkward, often exhilarating tango with numbers, goals, and dreams.

Let's Recap, No Financial Jargon

- We started by getting our bearings with The Compass Technique, because wandering in the financial wilderness without a map isn't a wise move. Remember, asking the right questions is half the battle.

- Then, we gently nudged with The Nudge Pact Technique, because sometimes we all need a little push to keep moving forward.

- Clear The Noise Technique swooped in like a superhero to rescue us from distraction and overwhelm. Cutting through the noise to focus on what matters? Yes, please.

- With The Explorer Technique, we ventured into uncharted territories of financial aspirations and fears. Turns out, X really does mark the spot.

- The Crowbar Technique showed us that tackling financial challenges head-on isn't as daunting as it seems.

- We took a long look in the mirror with The Mirror Moment Technique, reflecting on our actions and decisions without the emotional baggage.

- The Economic Echo Technique taught us that every decision has consequences, creating ripples that extend far beyond the initial splash.

- Finally, The Accolade Anchor Technique had us popping the champagne and celebrating our victories, because what's the point of hard work if you can't enjoy the successes?

So, What Now?

Now, it's time to apply these techniques to your financial plans with renewed purpose and strategy. Remember, financial planning isn't just about reaching a destination—it's about enjoying the journey and celebrating the milestones along the way.

And if there's one piece of advice I can leave you with, it's this: Be kind to yourself. Financial planning has its ups and downs, but as long as you keep moving forward, you're on the right track.

Here's to your financial journey—may it be as rewarding as it is enlightening. And when in doubt, refer back to these techniques. They're your compass, your map, and your telescope, guiding you through the financial seas toward the treasure chest of your dreams and goals.

Cheers to your success, and may your financial story be one for the books. Literally.

Cash Flow Mike

Appendix

The Elevation Sequence

Think of this as your cheat sheet for every stage of The Elevation Sequence. We're breaking down the techniques phase by phase, not just skimming the surface. We're talking about the what, the why, and the how-to of each technique, distilled into potent, actionable insights. It's like having a financial guru in your back pocket, ready to dispense wisdom on demand.

Harmony Phase: Here, we lay out the groundwork for building trust and alignment. We detail how The Compass Technique isn't just about asking questions—it's about asking the right questions. And let's not forget Clear The Noise, where we learn the art of focusing on what truly matters amidst the financial cacophony.

Depth Phase: Dive deeper with The Explorer and The Crowbar Techniques, equipped with strategies to unearth those hidden financial aspirations and fears. This section is your guide to probing beneath the surface, ensuring no stone is left unturned in the quest for financial clarity.

Elevate Phase: Ascend to new heights with The Economic Echo and The Accolade Anchor Techniques. We're talking about leveraging the past to fuel the future and celebrating victories as a springboard for next-level goals. This is where achievements are not just acknowledged but strategically utilized to propel forward.

Questions for Each Phase

The Compass– Navigating Emotional Landscapes

Description: Gently guides clients in opening up about their challenges, creating a safe space for sharing thoughts and feelings without fear of criticism, and building trust from the outset.

Sample Questions/Statements:

- Tell me what I'm looking at.
- What do you think happened to get to this point?
- What's something you wished others would understand about this situation?
- How can we explore this together, so you feel comfortable?

The Nudge Pact – Motivational Agreement Push

Description: Establishes a pre-agreed framework where clients identify signs indicating they're stuck and consent to receiving a motivational push towards action, fostering accountability and support.

Sample Questions/Statements:

- How will I know when you feel stuck?
- When you think about getting a nudge from me, what should I know?
- What's worked best for you in the past for encouragement? How do you think we should approach challenging topics?

Clear The Noise – Immediate Concerns First

Description: Allows the client to voice any immediate concerns or distractions at the beginning of a meeting, ensuring they feel heard and that their concerns are prioritized.

Sample Questions/Statements:

- What been going on in your world lately?
- Is there anything that you've been worried about lately?
- Is there anything you want to clear the air on before we start?
- I want to make sure we are focused on the most important things. What's that to you right now?

The Explorer– Discovery Through Inquiry

Description: Utilizes open-ended questions to help clients articulate their issues more clearly, facilitating a journey of discovery to uncover root causes and solutions.

Sample Questions/Statements:

- Tell me more about the situation.
- Why do you say think that is happening? Can you say that differently?
- What were you hoping would happen?

The Crowbar – Unearthing Deep Issues

Description: A technique designed to pry open the deeper issues within a company using a set pattern of questions, revealing underlying problems and themes for further exploration.

Sample Questions/Statements:

- What are we doing right?
- What feel like it's not working? What seems fuzzy right now?
- What is not here, but should be?
- What doesn't belong or doesn't fit?

The Mirror Moment – Reflective Behavioral Adjustment

Description: Holds up a metaphorical mirror to show clients the reflection of their actions, encouraging self-awareness and personal accountability.

Sample Questions/Statements:

- What stands out to you about that story?
- Is there anything you would change if you saw this pattern? How would you adjust your business in this situation?
- Does this behavior match the vision you have for your business?

The Economic Echo – Financial Insights Into Action

Description: Economic Echo is a technique that amplifies the importance of financial data in guiding strategic decisions and actions. It revolves around illustrating the tangible outcomes of financial choices, using data-driven insights to echo the potential for growth, efficiency, and profitability. This approach empowers clients to visualize the direct impact of their financial strategies, facilitating a more informed, proactive stance towards business development.

Sample Questions/Statements:

- Based on this financial data, what should we do next?
- Does seeing the numbers like this change the way you think about your strategy?
- Based on this snapshot, what stands out to you?
- Can you identify any financial trends that point towards an opportunity for action?

The Accolade Anchor – Celebratory Success Markers

Description: Creates memorable markers of success that serve as anchors for positive reinforcement, solidifying confidence and drive.

Sample Questions/Statements:

- Let's look at a recent win, what does that say about your strengths?
- How did it feel when you achieved that?
- How can we use this as a foundation for our next goal? What is the biggest lesson we learned during the process?

The Elevation Sequence

HARMONY

The Compass

The Nudge Pact - PRE

Clear The Noise

DEPTH

The Explorer

The Crowbar

The Mirror Moment

Clear PATH To Cash

WHAT TYPE OF ISSUE DID YOU FIND?

Education | Profit | Cash Flow | Debt | Operations | Future

ELEVATE

The Accolade Anchor

The Nudge Pact - POST

The Economic Echo

141

Made in the USA
Monee, IL
23 August 2024

64467794R00079